Lincolnshire
COUNTY COUNCIL

discover libraries

This book should be returned on or before the due date.

in
ead
und

N D I

vas
me
ien
ing
red

the
ke!

To renew or order library books please telephone 01522 782010
or visit https://lincolnshire.spydus.co.uk

You will require a Personal Identification Number.
Ask any member of staff for this.

The above does not apply to Reader's Group Collection Stock.

D0682477

HOLY SMOKE!

JILL DUDLEY
TRAVELS IN TURKEY
AND EGYPT

First published by
Orpington Publishers 2007, *reprinted* 2009
info@orpingtonpublishers.co.uk

Origination,
Cover Design and
Illustrations by
Clare E. Taylor
www.createabilitystudio.co.uk

Printed by
J F Print Ltd.,
Sparkford, Yeovil.

ISBN-13: 978-0-9553834-1-0

CONTENTS

In my book *Ye Gods!* I explored the ancient sanctuaries of the old Greek gods and the early Byzantine churches, and examined the manner in which some of the old pagan customs became absorbed into Christianity. In *Holy Smoke!* I have widened my field of vision to look, not only at the pagan gods and Christianity, but Judaism and Islam too.

On all the trips I have been accompanied by Harry, my husband, who has been a sort of anchor man to me, remaining true to his Christian upbringing and taking Christianity on trust, whilst leaving me to range freely in my search for answers to impossibly difficult questions.

This book is also a way for those who have no knowledge of Islam to learn something of the stories and legends of the Moslem faith, many of which have fascinating roots in Judaism.

PAGANS, CHRISTIANS & MOSLEMS

CHAPTER

1

ISTANBUL

It was after midnight when our taxi left Istanbul's international airport to join the speeding traffic alongside the Sea of Marmara. Our driver pointed to the flood-lit ancient city ramparts, and a little later to the multiple-domed Blue Mosque flanked by its minarets which, under its flood-lighting, rose spectacularly against the night sky. Then it vanished as the taxi took a left turn and plunged into a dark maze of narrow streets flanked by small wooden Turkish houses.

Despite our late night, I was elated when I was awoken at dawn by a muezzin calling the citizens to prayer - in fact by two of them yelling out 'Allahu Akbar' (God is Great) and other exhortations. We had at last arrived in Moslem Istanbul which had formerly been Christian Constantinople, and before that pagan Byzantium.

"So what's the plan for today?" Harry asked at breakfast. We were seated on the terrace of our hotel, looking out over roof tops to where ships sailed to and from the Bosphorus. I could just make out dolphins arching out and back into the water and thought immediately of

Apollo to whom once the dolphin had been sacred.

"Agia Sophia, of course!" I replied. "And the Blue Mosque."

"Hum."

"And – " But I stopped as I knew better than to list everything I hoped to do and see. The success of any trip with Harry rested mainly on his knowing nothing much, only how soon he would be home again. He tended to complain that the days abroad were action-packed and thank God he'd stopped me taking weeks, ignoring the fact that it was only because he wouldn't give me weeks that so much had to be packed into the time.

Immediately after breakfast we set out.

"'Scuse me, where you from?" We'd walked no more than twenty metres when a friendly voice from behind accosted us. We turned and saw a charming Turk in jeans and open neck shirt smiling at us.

"From England," I replied. Harry never speaks to foreigners if he can avoid it.

"Ah, England. England very nice. You want carpet?"

We always travelled light and the last thing we wanted was a carpet. We smiled politely and expressed our sorrow but no, we didn't want one.

We walked on along a public area filled with seats for those wanting to admire the Blue Mosque in one direction with its majestic pile of domes and, in the other, the equally magnificent basilica church of Agia Sophia with its wide central dome surrounded by semi-domes and smaller, shallower ones. Its four tall and slender minarets at each corner marked its conversion from church to mosque in the fifteenth century.

We headed first for the Blue Mosque. It had been built by the Sultan Ahmet I at the start of the seventeenth century. Because of its proximity to the Topkapi Palace the sultans had used it for their Friday prayers. The splendour of the imperial procession had been the highlight of the week for the people of the city.

Outside its entrance we had to pass a group of moustached characters selling picture postcards. As I was uncertain that my camera was working properly, I was keen to buy postcards depicting the main landmarks of Istanbul. Spotting my interest at once, a pleasant young man opened a concertina pack of cards before me like a conjurer. They were of Agia Sophia, the Blue Mosque and the Topkapi Palace and I liked them.

"To you four million lira," said the smiling Turk. A million Turkish lira was roughly the equivalent of one pound sterling. He saw me hesitating as I looked at the pictures. "Where you from?" enquired the friendly face. "Ah, from England! England very nice place. Three million five hundred thousand - nowhere so cheap."

"All right. Thank you."

He was well satisfied and leaned over me as I began counting out the notes - one million, two million... His hand came out towards the money. " 'Scuse me, this one - " and the hand somehow withdrew five million. "It is correct. You will not regret."

"Just a minute! You said three million five hundred thousand!"

"It is good. I have it here. No, no, not three million five hundred thousand. You have a bargain, five million. Thank you. England, it is very nice." The note had already been stowed away in his inside jacket pocket. The man was so agreeable it was impossible not to admire his guile. Five million, three million, seven million - What was money? Money was there to be spent, there to be taken. Money? Pooooh!

Feeling slightly cheated, but glad to have been of help to some poor fellow - and also ignoring Harry's 'Just what you'd expect from a foreigner' hiss in my ear - we entered the mosque, carrying our shoes in plastic bags provided for the purpose.

The Blue Mosque (also known as the Sultan Ahmet Camii) is so-called for its blue Iznik tiles with Islamic designs which decorate the inside walls and massive columns. The many arched, stained glass windows of blues, yellows and reds, all refracted the light.

We stood obediently behind a low brass railing which separated those who had come to look from those who had come to pray. Near to us was a tour guide, a pleasant tolerant-of-the-liberal-west young Turk, who was recounting the wonders of Islam to an American group. I overheard him say how etiquette demanded that, when a Moslem was at prayer, it was impolite to walk in front of him because it might distract him from his devotions, and he would then have to repeat his prayers. Moslem women were segregated from the men because of the distraction danger.

"As you can imagine," said the tolerant-of-the-liberal-west young Turk, determined to appear both easy-going and informative, "to have a woman bowing to Allah a few inches from your eye is not good for the man who prays to Allah, and he must begin his prayers over again. So it is better they are separate. Excuse me - please!" The tolerant-of the-liberal-west young Turk was speaking to me. "You are of this group?"

"No, no. I was just listening," I said hastily. "It is very interesting."

The mild admonishment for eavesdropping prompted me to look up at the spacious dome whilst remaining where I was. Harry edged away, distancing himself from a wife who was becoming an embarrassment.

"You now have questions for me?" enquired the guide.

"Can you tell us something about Moslem women?" asked a female voice.

"Yes, of course. Contrary to the opinion in the west, Moslem women have more freedom than it is believed. To us Moslems it is the man who is the head of the family and the woman who is the heart. Where is the body without the heart? Exactly! This shows to you how much we in Islam respect our women."

"So what about this polygamy thing?"

"Yes, let me answer you that. Firstly, let me say to you it is very important that the man can afford more than one wife. I wonder if you know that Muhammed himself had thirteen wives?"

"Thirteen? Is that a fact?"

"It is because he is the Prophet this is allowed. You may think that thirteen, even four, is too big a number, but you must allow for the cultural difference. At that time there are many battles and fatalities and, therefore, there are widows with children left. It is thought right and true to the spirit of Islam to take such widows and their children into the home for their protection. It is the law of Islam to take care of the weak."

"Do you have weddings like ours?"

"All that is needed for a marriage to be lawful is to sign a contract. Yes, of course, we have afterwards big celebrations such as feasting and dancing. Perhaps it is a surprise to you if I say that when a young woman she marries, her most important possession she takes with her to her new home is not her washing-machine, or her refrigerator, or her new saucepan, it is her prayer mat? This is the most important thing for her because all her prayers and feelings go into her mat. If her husband he walks with his shoes on her mat, this is an offence to his wife. It is the most bad thing that a husband can do to his wife for him to walk on her prayer mat."

"Except beat the wife, I guess?" quipped one.

"Or beat the mat?" guffawed another.

"Hush, dear!"

"I speak very seriously," admonished the tolerant-of-the-liberal-west young Turk. "No man must walk on the prayer mat of his wife. It is a big offence to her." He looked at his watch and held out an arm to move them on.

We too left the Blue Mosque and headed for Agia Sophia. The wide pathway was lined with Turkish women selling head scarves and men selling musical pipes. They advanced on us hopefully but we neither wanted scarves nor pipes. We were learning to keep our eyes to the ground, looking neither to left nor right. It was a pity because I really wanted to stare everywhere at this great city which straddled Europe and Asia and was a combination of both eastern and western influences.

Apparently, the Emperor Constantine, who first founded the city naming it Constantinople, originally thought of building his new capital at Troy. According to legend, however, he was led to the mouth of the Bosphorus by a flight of eagles. It was believed that Zeus, supreme god of the Olympian gods, used eagles as omens. Constantine was a great believer in being guided by omens and portents. I myself always feel absurdly encouraged when I see a black cat cross my path, or two magpies, or the new moon.

"Complete balderdash," Harry always says. "You can't seriously suppose it makes a blind bit of difference?"

"Well, it makes me feel optimistic."

"You're much more sensible than that."

"You think?"

With both Christianity and pagan gods in mind the Emperor Constantine prudently dedicated his greatest church in this, his new Christian city, to Agia Sophia. Agia Sophia means 'Holy Wisdom' which, to his pagan subjects, would reflect Athena, goddess of wisdom, and to Christians the holy wisdom of God. He also had coins struck with the head of Athena on one side and his own on the other. In those early days, although he recognized Christianity as a true religion, he adroitly hedged his bets regarding pagan gods and Christianity, not wanting to fall foul of either.

Inside Agia Sophia small arched windows let in muted light around the great central dome. The original depiction of Christ in the dome had, under Islam, been overlaid by a layer of plaster on which were now the finest artistic designs and words from the Koran. I tried rather hopelessly to unravel some of the Arabic script thinking that, after a winter studying the language, the secrets of Islam might be revealed to me. Large round black discs hung from the gallery and the gold calligraphy danced from right to left across them in pirouettes, whirls and arabesques. The discs proclaimed the names of Muhammed and the first Caliphs of the Moslem world.

I followed the pointing finger of a dapper looking Turkish guide wearing a dark suit as he translated the words in the dome to an American couple. The elderly husband stared upwards through his thin rimmed spectacles, his mouth half open in a sort of snarl, his knees slightly bent as though he were seated on an invisible stool.

"...the true and sublime words received by the Prophet Muhammed from Allah. Now I translate for you!" said the guide. "'In the name of God the Merciful and Compassionate. God is the light of Heaven and Earth. His light is Himself, not that which shines through glass or gleams in the morning star or glows in the fire.'"

"Wow! Don't you think that's just the finest script?"

"And they do it with a brush?"

"With the will of Allah," said the guide solemnly.

We went up a wide stone ramp to the gallery, once used by mounted horsemen. From there we had a good view of the apse and the mosaic portrayal of the Virgin Mary holding the infant Jesus on her lap. She was flanked by two angels whose huge flecked wings reached to their feet. To the Moslems Mary was the revered virgin mother of Jesus.

Muhammed was forty when he was enlightened. He'd been in the habit of taking himself off alone to a cave outside Mecca, and it was there in the month of Ramadan (which is why Ramadan is of importance to Moslems) that the angel Gabriel came to Muhammed and told him to recite the words he saw before him. As Muhammed was illiterate he was unable to obey the command. The angel embraced him and again ordered him to recite, but still he was unable to. The angel then held him so tightly that all the breath was squeezed from his body and he was ordered this time to say the words aloud after Gabriel. This he did, and the words became so deeply engraved on his heart that from then on he was able to recite them to others who put pen to paper. So the Koran was written word for word, sura (chapter) by sura. Many of the chapters reflect the life of Muhammed as he struggled to bring these revelations to the Arabs.

In the seventh century Moslems, inspired by the words of the Koran, and believing themselves to have the power of Allah with them, swept up from Arabia spectacularly conquering all before them. Constantinople, however, didn't capitulate until the fifteenth century.

I thought ruminatively how, at the time, the people of Constantinople had crowded into this great basilica church beseeching God.

"Isn't it odd," I said to Harry, "that when Jews, Christians and Moslems go to war with each other, they all call on God to save them? It must put God in a bit of a quandary as to who to support?" By now we were down from the gallery, seated on a ledge beside a huge alabaster jar. Harry was more concerned with easing the heel of his shoe to stop it from pinching. To him the present problem of having to get around Istanbul with a blister, was of much greater importance than whose side God was on in religious battles.

Agia Sophia had once been pillaged by the Roman Catholics who had grown to hate the Eastern Orthodox Church who, in its turn, loathed them. The Church had split when the Pope began making autocratic decisions regarding Church affairs. In the first centuries of Christianity all important Church matters had been decided by Patriarchs and bishops together. The final crunch had come when the Catholic west set out on the Fourth Crusade. Side-tracking from their goal of re-capturing Jerusalem from the Moslems, they had marched on Constantinople and out of sheer spite, in order to teach the Orthodox east a lesson for not following Rome's example in all things, they had arrived at Agia Sophia and had behaved as atrociously as only demented human beings can, wrecking, looting, raping and committing every sin deserving of hell-fire.

"Christianity really went off the rails then," I said, after informing Harry of the incident. "God must have been appalled!"

"Often war brings people back to God," came the vague reply. Harry's mind was still more on his shoe than on faith.

"But it's often because of God that wars are fought," I objected.

"You have to blame humans for that."

"That's easy to say!" I was incensed. "People are always excusing God and blaming humans! It was God who in the first place chose the Jews, then the Gentiles and, finally, the Moslems!"

But Harry was not to be drawn. The majestic building of Agia Sophia with its thick stone walls remained serenely impassive, whilst the possibility of a heated argument between husband and wife about God, faith and belief flared up, and then as quickly fizzled out.

The next day found us following a black moustached figure dressed in smart black trousers and jacket, a white shirt and a gaudy striped tie. He loped along side streets, leading us from the offices of Agia Sophia to the smaller, ancient domed Church of Agia Eirene (Holy Peace). The church was normally closed to the public but was sometimes opened if requested.

I had asked at the Agia Sophia offices to be allowed to see it and, after much ruminating and shaking of heads, the officials had finally relented, realizing that with certain stubborn English women it was easier to open the church than not to.

Agia Eirene was, in fact, the first church built by Constantine in this his Christian city. We approached the small domed building where our moustached character inserted a large key into the lock of the heavy oak, iron-studded door, lifted the iron bar securing it, and let us in. He spoke very limited English and pointed to his watch: "Twenty minutes. Close."

"Yes, yes. Thank you."

"Close - twenty minutes."

It was dark inside with shafts of light entering from its arched, leaded-paned windows in the dome. The electricity was switched on and a large black cross was revealed in the apse. Really, only its history could inspire images and fill the mind. The bare stone walls and flagged floor needed only twenty minutes.

I was interested in this church because, despite its dedication to 'Holy Peace', it had in fact witnessed some of the most violent scenes in the history of Christianity. During what was to become known as the Arian dispute in the fourth century, three thousand people had lost their lives there.

"And all because some man called Arius was arguing that God, as Father, must be transcendent and superior to Jesus," I told Harry. "Poor Arius and his supporters had to argue his point with Athanasius and others who were entrenched in the opinion that Jesus was of the same substance as God. In this day and age it's quite impossible to imagine the heart-searchings and hand-wringings that went into the making of what has become known as The Nicene Creed."

"So who won?" As far as Harry was concerned it mattered little.

"Not Arius. It was finally decided by the bishops at the Council of Nicaea, that Jesus was of the same substance as the Father."

"Oh."

"Don't you think it odd how congregations today rattle off the Creed quite unaware of the agonizings that went into its construction? How many people know that once people were prepared to riot and die for the inclusion or exclusion of this or that word. Amazing!"

We climbed a wide balustraded stairway to a gallery and began to wonder what next to look at, so came down again.

Seeing the door ajar, a lone woman in her thirties, wearing a well cut red jacket and carrying a small haversack, entered. She had dark, curly hair and an intelligent face, and began to look around with an open guide-book in her hand. Moustache appeared and tried to usher her out again - she was not part of his brief. She appealed to us, speaking in English with a foreign accent.

"It is not allowed? I want only to look."

I explained that we'd been given special permission but couldn't see why she shouldn't join us. She was clearly no vandal. I made gestures to Moustache that she was acceptable and he backed off with a resigned shrug.

The woman wandered off alone and then returned to tell us about panels of mosaics arrayed along a vaulted quadrangle at the back. But we couldn't tell what age they were or where they were from. Anyway Moustache came and pointed to his watch again. He was very authoritative and we didn't like to abuse the privilege of having had the church opened for us.

Once outside and with Moustache gone, the young woman told us she was from Holland and had been travelling alone for two months, exploring Armenia and Georgia. She was a lawyer but had felt the need to take a break from the demands made on her, so had packed her bags and set off.

"And you?" she enquired.

I told her that Harry was a semi-retired farmer, and I was a writer interested in the monotheistic religions and how they'd emerged from the pagan past. Then I told her we were about to take a taxi to the Patriarchate a little way up the Golden Horn. There the Patriarch would be taking the Good Friday morning service. Would she like to come?

Oh, yes, she would. What an unexpected turn of events for her. She hadn't thought it possible to see the Patriarch. But Easter? Wasn't Easter over?

I explained that in the Orthodox Church Easter was celebrated according to the old Julian calendar. This could make Easter sometimes several days or even weeks out of line with the Gregorian calendar used by the west.

We took a taxi and were driven at speed along the Golden Horn towards the Patriarchate. After about ten minutes the taxi turned left and put us down at the bottom of an extremely steep and narrow cobbled street. The driver pointed up to a red brick building at the top and told us that that was the Patriarchate. We paid him several million lira (equivalent to about two pounds) and decided that taking cheap taxis and getting around, was preferable to waiting for buses and being put down far from where we wanted to be.

We walked up the steep cobbled street, past poverty stricken houses strung with washing. A large solid, black painted entrance gate was crowned by a red brick archway which had on it in Greek lettering the word 'Patriarchate'. I pressed the bell repeatedly but received no response. Knowing that there had to be a Good Friday service going on, we made enquiries from various people but nobody spoke English or seemed to know about churches. Workmen, digging up cobbles higher up this narrow street, carelessly (or deliberately) let them tumble down towards us so we had to dodge them. The Dutch woman examined her guide-book and told us that the black gate had to be the one which was now kept sealed, because it was where the Patriarch had been hanged for treason at the outbreak of the Greek War of Independence in the nineteenth century. During Greece's bid for freedom the Orthodox Church had played its part, and the public hanging of the Patriarch must have been a fearful warning to all Orthodox Christians not to rebel against Turkish (Moslem) rule.

We eventually made enquiries at a police station and were pointed in the right direction to the Church of St. George. Chanting could be heard as we approached. I was sorry we wouldn't be seeing more of the Dutch woman, but we had to say good-bye outside as as she was flying home that afternoon and could only stay a short while.

We entered and stood amongst the crowded congregation of Greek ex-patriots living in what they still prefer to call Constantinople. The smell of incense hung on the air. There were numerous lighted candles, icons and a carved and gilded sanctuary screen (iconostasis). Several young black-bearded priests in their black cassocks and caps stood beside the bishop's throne. On it sat the imposing figure of the grey-bearded Patriarch, holding his patriarchal pastoral staff. He had a scarlet and gold chasuble over his black cassock and wore the black patriarchal head-dress draped at the back with the long black veil.

The chanting became mournful as a cloth, embroidered with the figure of Christ, was carried in procession around the church, together with tall candles tied with mauve ribbons and the Gospels in a gold encrusted cover. The embroidered cloth was then laid on the large rectangular Epitaphios (a representation of Christ's tomb, decorated with small white flower heads) placed centrally before the Royal Doors to the sanctuary screen. Reverently, the Patriarch stood before it and scattered rose petals over it.

It was odd to think that this annual Good Friday service commemorated an event two thousand years ago, yet another occasion when fanatically held beliefs had led to violence and misery. Because the signs had not been right, the majority of Jews had felt compelled to deny that Jesus was their expected Messiah. A minority had been as convinced that he was. The Romans, who only honoured the pagan deities had, finally, lost all patience with the lot of them. As for Jesus himself, he'd led his exemplary life fulfilling what he believed to be God's will and purpose. But why, as a consequence, had there been so much conflict and division? Had God got it wrong or, as Harry would say, it was only men who got things wrong?

The Good Friday service was coming to an end and soon a queue was forming to go up to the Epitaphios. I noticed people coming away from the Patriarch carrying flowers, and I joined the queue, thinking that my fog of incomprehension regarding Christianity might suddenly clear under the watchful eye of the Patriarch.

Harry was not into such mysteries being a thorough Protestant, or protester, so abandoned me to my search for enlightenment. The advance was slow but, as I drew near, I saw that those ahead made the sign of the cross, kissed the face of Christ on the Epitaphios, then the Gospels and then the hand of the Patriarch. My turn was upon me and I braced myself to do the right thing, hoping I wouldn't be spotted as an English heathen and cast by the Patriarch into outer darkness.

I kissed the face of Christ and immediately was aware of a rose petal sticking to my lip. I quickly removed it before kissing the Gospels. I supposed I should return the rose petal but, instead, hung on to it thinking I would keep it as a memento. Thief! The Patriarch had his bouquet of flowers ready consisting of two stalks of white flowers. I kissed the patriarchal hand, and received the stalks feeling strangely humble, though this soon turned to triumph as I turned away.

Outside I found Harry waiting patiently.

"Not exactly a bridal bouquet," he remarked.

I looked at my two stalks and felt absurdly pleased with them. "A simple symbolic gesture of goodwill," I said.

"Well, there you are! You're always looking for factual truth, when symbolism is all you need."

I looked at him critically. Was that what it was all about, just symbolism?

As it was Friday and the Islamic day of prayer we took a taxi on to the Eyup mosque, an important sacred centre for Moslems further up the Golden Horn. After a ten minute drive we found ourselves beside a narrow road of small shops thronged with people. We got out and joined the crowds. Many women ambled along clutching the hands of small children and carrying shopping bags. They all had their heads covered and wore long coats over their dresses.

We entered the outer cobbled courtyard to the mosque where the women were gathered on seats, idly gossiping. It was like a great picnic as some opened bags and began to munch their lunch. They appeared very content on this their day out with the family, not one looked as though her husband had walked on her prayer mat.

I hoped to see inside the mosque, so we pressed forward until we were stopped by a couple of armed police. I said I only wanted to see and they waved us on with their guns. We entered another courtyard where there was a canopied ablutions fountain surrounded by a seat; here men sat washing their faces, hands and feet before going on to their devotions.

The mosque was the holiest in Istanbul, and one of the most important in the Islamic world. It marked the place where the standard bearer and companion of Muhammed, whose name was Eyup Ensari, lost his life in the first Arab siege of Constantinople in the seventh century. It was made a condition of the peace treaty that followed, that Eyup Ensari would be forever honoured and his tomb preserved. When Constantinople fell to the Ottoman Turks in the fifteenth century, the Sultan Mehmet built the mosque to his memory. From then on it was to this mosque that sultans came to be girded with the sword of Osman (the equivalent for sultans of a coronation).

We felt conspicuous in this crush of Moslem

worshippers as we moved forward towards the inner courtyard. The Imam's homily was being relayed to those outside. In that inner courtyard a few men first paid their respects to a high arched brass grid in a wall recess, surrounded by vivid blue designs of Iznik tiles in four different panels, before attending to their prayers to Allah. I supposed the grid was the shrine to Eyup Ensari.

More large prayer mats were brought by attendants who unrolled them outside the mosque as worshippers began to overflow into the courtyard. It was then that I suddenly noticed I was the only woman there.

I didn't like to stay longer in this male province, where already men were taking to the newly unrolled prayer mats, performing the required ritual of standing, then kneeling and prostrating themselves to Allah. We surreptitiously did a bolt and felt more at ease when we were back in the outer bazaar with its many small shops.

Up the hill behind the mosque was the cemetery of Eyup. Higher still there was a superb view of the Golden Horn. Local legend has it that Zeus, (supreme Olympian god), fell in love with Io, a priestess at a temple of Hera (Zeus' wife) and, to protect her from the fury of his jealous wife, he turned her into a heifer. Hera, however, found out and set a gadfly on Io which so tormented the poor girl-come-priestess-come-heifer, that she was driven all over the world by it. She ended up at Eyup where she gave birth to a daughter, Cereossa. The story goes that Poseidon, god of the sea, then fell in love with Cereossa and, as a result, she gave birth to Byzas who founded Byzantium, the small town which was to become Constantinople. To extend the story to even greater lengths, it has been suggested that the Golden Horn gets its name from Cereossa, which may be a corruption of the Greek word 'chrysos' meaning gold; the 'horn' part of it comes from her mother Io, the heifer, who presumably had golden horns.

"I love the stories of the old pagan gods," I said to Harry, as we hung around hopefully for a taxi to take us back. "The old gods were never holier than thou. In fact, were considerably unholier than anyone."

"It's rather more easy to have one God, I'd say," came the reply.

"I don't know. If there are a number of them then, if you fall foul of one, you can appeal to another. After all, Constantine didn't altogether abandon the old gods. He just took on board the God of the Christians, and the Christians then piled on the pressure."

"Pressure?" queried Harry.

"Of God's wrath and vengeance and the awful Day of Judgement and all that. Do you know that, despite all his Christianizing of things, Constantine didn't get baptized until he was on his death-bed? A Roman Catholic I spoke to said that in those days people didn't. But that's not true because those who wanted to become Christian were immediately baptized into the faith. Can you imagine Constantine's dilemma? Not wanting to offend Apollo or Zeus or any of the other gods, whilst acknowledging the Christian God? Some have even suggested that he got baptized when close to death in order to be washed clean of his numerous sins which included several murders concerning members of his family. In this way he would, so he gambled, arrive as a pure soul before God. Although, I can't see why, if you're riddled with sin, being baptized should wash it all away. But Constantine was hedging his bets as usual."

A taxi containing a family of Moslems drew up conveniently nearby and disgorged its passengers. We quickly hurried over. I was getting used to being taken around in taxis and, because of his blister, Harry for once wasn't complaining about extravagance.

I asked the driver if he knew what I meant by the Çemberlitas Column. "Çemberlitas? Yes, yes." We sped along the Golden Horn noting that his speedometer was fixed at thirty however fast he went. We drew up in a busy thoroughfare and the driver pointed to the word 'Çemberlitas' on a building.

"No, no, not Turkish bath. Column," I said. "You wouldn't like a Turkish bath, would you?" I asked Harry, and received the expected reply. "What? Sit half-naked with a lot of Turks? No fear!"

The taxi continued at a crawl (though still showing thirty on the speedometer). He drew up near a paved area and pointed to a column that looked like the stump of a factory chimney. "Çemberlitas," he said.

"That's it!" It was as though I'd just spotted a long lost child.

"That's what?"

"The Column of Constantine - well, what remains of it. You just have to use your imagination."

We got out and walked around the monument. A couple of benches for tired tourists made us fair game for shoeshine boys. They vied with each other to polish Harry's shoes. I had open sandals so had nothing to polish. Harry tucked his feet under the bench and said 'Shoo!' which to the boys meant an invitation to polish 'shoe'. They dived around trying to pull his feet forward. It seemed best to get up and walk. The boys were crestfallen but were soon drawn to other quarries with leather shoes.

"What's special about this thing?" Harry asked.

I told him how it had been the crowning glory of Constantine's new city, and had been erected to commemorate the dedication of Constantinople as his new capital in 330 A.D. For the celebrations Constantine had had a mix of Christian and pagan priests and Christian and pagan rites. The area had been a forum with columned porticoes, statues of emperors, pagan gods and Christian saints. Atop the hundred foot column had been a statue of Constantine.

"The interesting thing being," I went on, "that for the statue Constantine took the body of Apollo - one sculpted by the great Phidias who was responsible for the Parthenon marbles - and put a sculpture of his own head on it wearing a radiate crown. In one hand he held a sceptre, and in the other a globe." I led Harry around the remaining stump of the column. "Constantine's radiate crown represented the sun - not forgetting that Apollo was once equated with the sun."

To mark the occasion, Constantine also buried Christian and pagan relics in the column's twenty foot marble plinth. There were said to be nails from Christ's crucifixion, together with fragments of the True Cross and Mary Magdalene's jar of ointment - all brought from Jerusalem by Constantine's pious mother Helena. For the benefit of pagans there were rays from Apollo's crown, and the palladium of Athena. According to the second century travel writer, Pausanius, the palladium had been the most sacred possession of Athens having fallen from heaven. Greek and Roman belief was that the safety of a city depended on its presence.

"Can you imagine the forum here?" I asked.

"Can't imagine anything," said Harry, as traffic hurtled along the nearby street and another shoeshine boy spotted us.

Oh, well. On to the Topkapi, then.

The Topkapi Palace was built in the mid-fifteenth century by the Sultan Mehmet (Mehmet the Conqueror). For this palatial project he chose the promontory where the Sea of Marmara converged with the Golden Horn.

The grandeur and wealth of the Ottoman Empire was revealed as we walked through these extensive buildings. Every object, from thrones to egg-cups, was richly decorated and bejewelled or wrought in precious metals.

After humming and hawwing with admiration and astonishment that so much money could be lavished on the humblest of items, we moved on to the building which housed the sacred relics. Here were objects which, under normal circumstances, would be vacuumed up or given away but, from the spiritual point of view, were priceless and, therefore, exhibited in gold wrought and jewel-studded containers. A hair from Muhammed's beard, for example; a piece of broken tooth, his bamboo bow, swords, mantel and many suchlike things. Of great significance was his footprint, said to have appeared in stone from where the Prophet had ascended to heaven in Jerusalem, now marked by the Al Aqsa Mosque. The broad imprint in stone was displayed in a gold box.

The story of Muhammed's ascension is unusual. One night the angel Gabriel had woken Muhammed from a deep sleep and shown him a winged and brilliantly shining creature which looked something like a mule. He was told to sit astride this beast whose name was Buraq. Each stride Buraq took reached to the horizon. Eventually, Muhammed was put down at Jerusalem on the site of Solomon's temple. There Muhammed was met by other prophets of Islam - two of these were prophets of the Old

Testament, Abraham and Moses, and the third was Jesus. Muhammed prayed with them before sitting astride his shining Buraq and being taken up through the six heavens where he met the prophets again including Adam, and on to the seventh heaven, where he was left by Gabriel to enter God's presence. Some say Muhammed saw the face of Allah, others that it was his heart alone which felt him to be there.

God commanded Muhammed to see to it that Moslems prayed fifty times a day. Muhammed accepted this calmly but, when Moses heard, he told him to return to Allah and request a lesser burden to be put on his people since, in his own experience, he had found it difficult to persuade the Israelites to pray at all. After repeated returns to Allah, the number of daily prayers were reduced gradually from fifty to forty, then thirty until, finally, five times daily was agreed. Even five Moses warned was excessive, but Muhammed didn't like to ask Allah to reduce it further.

"Good God!" said Harry, when he heard this story, "to have a call to prayer fifty times a day! That would mean every half hour. Down on your knees every time you've milked six cows! Can you imagine it?"

We continued along the exhibits of the holy relics until we came to a turban in a glass case, said to be from the Prophet Isuf. In my by now bemused state, I took the 'f' in Isuf to be the Old English way of writing 's', and so supposed it was the Turkish word for Jesus, though I couldn't imagine Jesus in a turban.

By this time we felt saturated by overkill and over-achievement and had no desire to see any more wonders. As our hotel was nearby we started to walk back. On the way I told Harry how odd it was to be in this Moslem city with the Orthodox Church celebrating Christ's death, crucifixion and Resurrection when, in the Koran, God revealed to Muhammed that the Christians had got it quite wrong and Jesus hadn't been crucified at all, it was merely thought that he had been. We were deafened suddenly by the call to prayer from a nearby muezzin. There was no respite for several minutes as another joined in. We were caught in the cross-fire as each responded to the other.

Silence, or rather a return to the noise of traffic.

"So how do you explain that?" I asked.

"Explain what?"

"That God enlightened Muhammed to say that Jesus hadn't been crucified, and he hadn't died and been buried, but had been lifted up by God to himself. Or something like that."

"Well, obviously Moslems don't want to see things the Christian way because they want to be different," said Harry glibly.

"So God, after all the agonizings of his Christians to get their doctrines right, made it known to an Arab in the Arabian desert that they had got it wrong? Couldn't he have put it in the Christian mind to get it right from the start?"

"Yes. No. Yes. Well - "

"'Scuse me, where you from?" A pleasant voice interrupted. But by now we knew better than to say anything. We were from nowhere, going nowhere and wanting nothing. We ignored the smiling face. "You want carpet? Please, you come with me. Carpet very cheap. I have shop very near. You look only."

We walked on, eyes to the ground. A quick fertive glance and I spotted a few yards further on a Turk standing in the doorway of his carpet shop. I saw across the road a delicatessen selling spices and we quickly crossed the road to it. Displayed in the window were the rich colours of cinnamon, saffron, paprika and other exotic products. We liked the look of the shop and went in. Inside was a polite young man who spoke English.

"Good evening. Can I help you?" he asked pleasantly.

After a great deal of indecision we bought packets of different spices, and boxes of Turkish delight. The young man wrapped everything up with care, and seemed so amiable that I thought I could ask him about Islam. It came out unexpectedly as a question about the Prophet Isuf's turban.

"Perhaps you can answer a question I have?" I began.

"If I can help, of course," he said most charmingly.

"Is the Prophet Isuf, Jesus?" He looked momentarily startled, and I explained this somewhat unexpected question. "In the Topkapi Palace there is a turban - you know, a hat - " I demonstrated the winding of material around the head, "of the Prophet Isuf. Is that Jesus?"

"No, it is the Prophet Joseph."

"Ah, Joseph! The father of Jesus!"

The young spice man looked more shocked and said at once: "Jesus had no father."

"Yes, he had."

"No."

"Joseph and Mary," I said

"No. He had no father."

"Oh, you mean Jesus was the Son of God?"

"It is this the Christians say."

Help! I was immediately aware of the strange double-think of Christianity. On the one hand Jesus was the Son of God, on the other Joseph was his human father, or wasn't. And yet Jesus was said to be descended from the house of David through Joseph. How could one be expected to believe this confusion except by not thinking at all?

"The Prophet Isuf is from Egypt."

"Oh, that Joseph!" I turned to Harry. "The Joseph from the Old Testament - the coat of many colours Joseph."

"Well, that's that cleared up then," said Harry reasonably.

I turned to the spice man. "So what do Moslems believe about Jesus?"

"He is one of the prophets of Allah. Mary is his mother. We have it written in our Koran: 'We (that is Allah) breathed of Our spirit into her, and made both her and her son as a sign for the Universe.'"

"Really?" I was fascinated by this young man who spoke so simply and from the heart. "So you think the Christians have it wrong?"

"We say that there is no other God but Allah. You cannot say he is three people as the Christians say."

"That makes sense," I said.

He looked at me in silence then, assessing that I wasn't there to pick a quarrel, said: "In the Koran it is written, 'believe in God and His apostles and do not say: "Three"... God is but one God. God forbid that He should have a son!'" He looked at me solemnly. "But you are Christian?" he asked.

"Well - yes, sort of. I'm interested in Islam," I explained.

He turned towards a world map he had on his wall and, pointing to it, said: "This shows the spread of Islam in the world." He indicated the countries coloured red, others that were pink and those left blank. "This red shows what is all Moslem, and this here is some Moslem. Here is no

Moslem. You can see how Islam is everywhere."

"Islam means 'submission' and 'peace'?" I asked.

"If you submit to the will of Allah, then you cannot do wrong. That gives you peace," said the young man.

As we left, I said to Harry: "Well, there you are! Perhaps I'll become a Moslem!"

"You? I can't see you down on your knees five times a day," came the prompt reply.

I could see the disadvantages and had to admit I couldn't see it either.

The next day, far from being a bright spring morning, it was foggy and wet, which put paid to our plans to go up the Bosphorus on a pleasure-steamer. The Sea of Marmara was blanketed and container ships looked like spectres whilst fog-horns sounded eerily.

Our apologetic-for-the-weather receptionist said we could do a guided tour by coach for the equivalent of eighteen pounds each. Harry wouldn't hear of such extravagance and, anyway, we'd seen many of the sights already. As the ferry-boats were still functioning, we took a taxi down to them and zigzagged across the Bosphorus through the fog for the equivalent of forty pence a trip.

Discovering the manner in which tickets were issued caused excitement. At the ticket office I paid the money and was given two coins in exchange but no tickets, whereupon I all but accused the poor man of stealing. This walrus-moustached character got me to empty out my purse; he retrieved the two coins he had given me and shook them at me in an 'Oh, foolish woman!' rebuke. "Tickets!" he said. Another individual from the long queue forming behind us showed extreme patience and told us to follow him. He demonstrated how the metal tokens had to be put into a slot at the turnstile to let us through to the ferry-boats. Once this had been achieved we made several triumphant trips, if not up the Bosphorus, at least across it, from Europe into Asia and back again.

It was on this famous waterway that Jason had once travelled with his Argonauts on his quest for the golden fleece. The golden fleece was a pagan story, not dissimilar to God's command to Abraham to sacrifice Isaac (Old Testament story), or his command to Abraham at Mecca to sacrifice Ishmael (Moslem story), then, satisfied that Abraham was willing to obey, had sent a ram to be sacrificed instead.

In the pagan story somebody was about to sacrifice two children in some sort of fertility rite but, in the nick of time, Zeus sent a ram with a golden fleece who rescued the two children. They climbed onto its back and the ram flew away with them. Not totally to be unexpected, one of the children fell off and was drowned, but the other reached Colchis on the Black Sea where he sacrificed the ram to Zeus, and its golden fleece became the object of discovery by Jason.

In those far off days men had had desperate adventures and had called on the gods and goddesses with as much faith as any Jew, Christian or Moslem today. Their hearts had been strengthened, and their souls inspired by belief in the Olympian deities.

By the time we'd finished zigzagging on the Bosphorus and had done a tour of the Dolmabahçe Palace, whose marble fronted exterior vied with its dripping-with-crystals interior, the weather had miraculously cleared. We returned to our hotel for a late siesta, in order to prepare ourselves for the Resurrection service we were going to attend that night under the watchful eye of the Patriarch.

"Christos anestei!" (Christ is risen!)

"Aleithos anestei!" (Truly he is risen!)

The Greek community were jam-packed around me and hailed each other with this Easter greeting. The crowds at this midnight Resurrection service parted to allow the Patriarch to pass through the Church of St. George to the courtyard. That night the Patriarch wore a glittering domed mitre and was followed by priests, nuns and monks. All had lighted candles. I held a candle, but the heat inside the church had melted it into a curve, and I hadn't lit it.

"An atheist?" said Harry when we squeezed our way out through the throng gathered around the Patriarch, who was by now delivering his Easter message from a dais in the courtyard. "I don't think you want to be an atheist."

"I don't want to be, but it's what I think I am." Despite all my hopes and expectations that somehow I'd have some divine revelation in the presence of the Patriarch, I had come to this conclusion. I was no longer a sceptic, or a wavering agnostic, I was an atheist. I expected to be struck dead, or incinerated by a flame from one of the numerous candles held by the faithful. Instead, I saw someone else's hair go up in smoke.

Somewhere in the Bible, and in the Koran too, I'd read that God sometimes pulled a veil down or hardened the hearts of people so they couldn't believe, and nothing could be done about it. As I was heavily veiled I'd play the atheist as clearly that's what God wanted.   Except as an atheist there was no God.

We found a taxi with a young Kurdish driver who was bursting with energy and joie de vivre.   Seeing my bent and unlighted candle, he seized it from me, broke off the offending hook, leapt from the driver's seat and accosted an astonished couple walking nearby and asked them to light it for him.   He returned to the car and handed me the 'Light of the world' which, in my present atheistic frame of mind, could be as much symbolic of Phoebos Apollo (Phoebos meaning 'shining', 'pure') as of Christ, or just a lighted candle which, of course, it was.

Was there so much difference between those who were pagan and those who were Christian - or those who weren't anything at all, for that matter? Well, according to the Old Testament, the New Testament and the Koran, the difference was heaven and everlasting bliss, or hell and eternal damnation.

Oh, God!

I changed 'Oh, God!' to 'Oh, well!' and set my jaw as I looked out of the window. Our driver was jolly and happy and drove at speed the wrong way up one-way streets in order to take short cuts; and around the wrong side of central islands, and through red traffic lights. We arrived back in record time amidst much laughter and a joyful sense of defying all authority. Divine retribution wasn't teaching me a lesson - not yet. And so, for the time being I played the atheist with no ill effects, and remained happily aloof from all scripture.

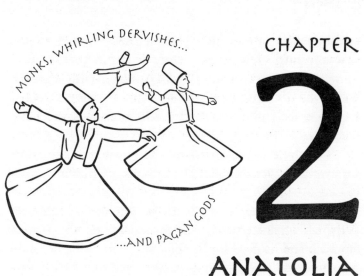

MONKS, WHIRLING DERVISHES...

...AND PAGAN GODS

CHAPTER

2

ANATOLIA

'May the God who called our father Abraham to journey into the unknown, and guarded him and blessed him, protect me too and bless my journey. May his confidence support me as I set out...' The Reverend's voice continued to recite this 'Prayer for Travellers'.

The coach stopped and started as it crawled its way through the suburbs of Ankara. The high hills of the city were stacked with shacks inhabited by the poor with domes and minarets of mosques rising here and there above them. In due course Ankara was left behind and the coach escaped like a rat from a trap and sped off along the open road heading south-east.

I was amazed at myself - perhaps annoyed would be a better word - because we were in an organized group. As neither of us spoke Turkish and the hassle of travelling independently was somewhat daunting with the great distances to be covered in Anatolia, Harry had insisted we join a conducted tour. On its itinerary were visits to early Byzantine churches as well as to certain pagan sites which I particularly wanted to see. It wasn't until a few weeks before departure that we were sent a 'spiritual itinerary', and I realized with alarm it was to be a Christian pilgrimage and we were expected to join in daily prayers and Holy Communions and Bible readings.

'For thine is the kingdom, the power and the glory, for ever and ever, Amen.' The murmur of English voices ceased.

Harry was very happy with the situation. To be on a British organized tour, which understood the British stomach and its need for hygiene, was something he could relax into and enjoy. For my part I tried to submit to my lot meekly. One half of me was quite pleased to be with dedicated Christians whose faith would surely protect us whilst driving on Turkish roads, the other half was feeling frustrated not to be travelling independently and more adventurously.

The Reverend was a kindly middle-aged man, concerned with the welfare and happiness of his group. 'Christian centred' were words that seemed to be most apt when describing him. Everything he did was done with faith and patience from the central point of belief. He was barrel chested, and had a healthy, cherubic pink face, grey hair and large brown eyes. He wore tropical shorts, open neck shirt and sandals, and carried a Bible.

Natasha, our guide, was a Turkish woman who spoke excellent English, and was fiercely determined to rewrite history in order to obliterate as much as possible anything about the early Greeks of Anatolia. After listening to her, I began to think I'd got it wrong in believing the Greeks had settled in Asia Minor before the Romans. I forebore questioning her about historical facts for fear of upsetting her; anyway, whenever I did ask some simple question she often ignored me altogether. I became aware that a barrier of mutual antipathy and suspicion was building up between us. As the coach bowled along she stood facing us, swaying to the movement of the coach, wide-eyed with scholarly information, a mike held against her bottom lip, one hand steadying herself as it grasped the back of the seat.

We drove for miles along the dead straight road, cutting across the vast hinterland of Anatolia as we headed for Cappadocia. Eventually a stretch of water to our right broke the monotony, and in the far distance a high snow-capped mountain drew everyone's attention. It was the extinct volcano Mount Erciyes, we were informed, and the stretch of water was one of several salt lakes.

The plateau continued to undulate before us in a featureless and treeless expanse; it looked uncultivated, but Natasha said defensively that it was farmed by individuals who lived in the villages, though we could see no village in this vast tract of land. It was not until some time later that the monotony of the landscape merged with a more cultivated area and turned to pasture. We passed the occasional flock of sheep guarded by ferocious looking dogs. Shepherds in baggy pantaloons stared at the passing coach. Large stones marked out the boundaries of ownership. Here we saw several villages consisting of a few small houses, each with a plot of ground with chickens, goats and donkeys. The occasional ancient tractor revealed signs of 'progress'.

As we approached Cappadocia the landscape changed again. Here were mushroom grey hills and rocks with numerous cavities in them. This was the area where fourth century Christians had set up monastic retreats. Today, thanks to the tourist industry, hotels were springing up everywhere. The buildings blended with the environment, many having small arched windows to resemble the old cave monasteries.

The bus drew up at our hotel. I had to admit there were advantages travelling in an organised tour as all luggage was carried for us, and there were no worries about tipping (or not tipping come to that).

The Reverend informed us that at 6.30 that evening he would hold a prayer meeting and afterwards he would outline the itinerary for the following day. Practising humility, conformity and being one of many sheep in a flock was tough. But if I was ever to understand Christianity it had to be now, travelling as we were under this Christian umbrella.

'Thou who knowest each one's need, and hast heard their prayer, grant unto each according to thy merciful loving kindness, and thy eternal love; through Jesus Christ, our Lord, Amen.' This was again followed by the Lord's Prayer.

It was 8.30 a.m. and we were already on our way to one of the major sites of Cappadocia, the Göreme Open Air Museum. Natasha gave us a brief history of how the Hittites, then the Persians, Alexander the Great (she didn't mention the Greeks) and then the Romans, the Christians and, finally, the Moslems had come into Anatolia. It was, however, the early Christians of Cappadocia who put the area on the historical map.

The landscape was a panorama of beige and grey tufaceous rock formations eroded by wind and rain. Gullies and ravines were filled with rocky pinnacles pitted with pigeon-holes or man-made caves in which Christian ascetics had taken up their abode. It is said that they were escaping Roman persecution. Equally, these ascetics believed that they were, by denying their bodily needs and comforts, preparing their souls for salvation.

"What exactly is salvation?" I asked Harry.

"Salvation? Well, it's something to do with salvaging, I suppose. Nobody wants to feel that when they die it's the end."

"A sort of recycling of the self?"

"I suppose so."

The monastic settlement in these Cappadocian rock caves had been encouraged by Basil the Great (St. Basil), who had become bishop of nearby Caesarea (today's Kayseri). I had asked the Reverend if we could do a detour to it as it was less than twenty-five miles away. He had waffled kindly, thought it sounded interesting and said he would consult Natasha and the driver. Whether he did I don't know, but we didn't go. My hope of nipping off alone in a taxi was somehow not possible either. Nobody but I knew how much forbearance I put into this trip in order not to upset the smooth running of the tour.

Before becoming a renowned Church leader Basil the Great had spent five years in Athens studying philosophy and rhetoric. In one of his numerous letters as bishop, he recommended the art of sophistry (the ability to make false things appear true and vice versa). Sophistry, St. Basil wrote, is a wonderful accomplishment, enabling a man to 'make great things small, whenever he so wishes, and to invest small things with greatness...'

"Perhaps that's why Christianity took off?" I suggested to Harry. "It was the art of persuading people to believe what is not, or not to believe what is obvious."

"I doubt that very much," Harry replied stolidly.

"I mean some Roman Catholics still believe that when you die you rise bodily to heaven when clearly you go into the ground."

"Nobody believes that any more."

"Some people do. But the very fact that they did once must, surely, mean that what was once believed was wrong from the start, or that God changes his mind from age to age. Or there's no God at all and we're all conned by sophistry?"

The subject came to a timely end as the coach drew up near the entrance to the Göreme Museum. The doors of the coach were opened and the Close Cropped Christians, as Harry and I called those from a church in Colchester with easy to manage short grey hair, were the first to clamber out; some of them were over eighty and were supported by sticks. I wondered how they would manage the long route and the uneven steps leading into some of the old churches and monastic dwellings.

Pinnacles, crags and eroded weird-shaped rocks reared up along the valley. Many had enticing cave entrances, some sculpted and arched whilst others were just oval holes. We were marshalled into an orderly group with Natasha leading like a small mis-shapen black crab scurrying ahead, and the Reverend following up behind.

Because we were a group we were not allowed into a monastic church until the tour group inside came out. Slowly we did the rounds of these strange habitations containing churches and chapels with their weathered frescoes and stone altars. Some doorways had carved lintels and pillars and capitals. The floors were of hard packed sandstone. Natasha informed us about the coenobite monks (monks who lived in a community, as opposed to hermits). She spoke about their farming practices, and pointed out the numerous small holes in the rock where they'd bred pigeons specifically to lay eggs whose yolks would be used for the painting of icons.

Know-it-all-been-everywhere, a woman in her fifties who had no companion, kept close to Natasha and began to talk about the journey she'd made to South America and her interest in the Incas, which was quite off the point. She realized that this was not the moment, and added quickly: "I'll tell you afterwards - sorry to interrupt!" We were in the vaulted roofed Tokali Kilisi (Church with the Buckle) which was hewn out of the rock around the tenth or eleventh century. It had four arched columns to the sanctuary and every wall was covered in a blue background with frescoed figures of saints and various scenes from the Old Testament. Amongst the frescoes were St. Basil and the Emperor Valens and a scene from the Council of Nicaea.

We moved on. "Gather round me, please!" Natasha's voice came from deep within yet another cave church. "We are now in the Yilanli Kilise which means the Church with the Snake. This is because, as you can see, we have here the two saints, St. George and St. Theodore. You all know the story of St. George and the dragon? Do any of you know about Theodore? He was, according to popular belief, a Roman soldier who was burned alive in the Pontus for his refusal to join with the army in worshipping the pagan gods. In the Eastern hagiography it is Theodore who first fought with the dragon, not St. George." Natasha's voice rose like a great operatic contralto to make herself heard. "Now, are there any questions?"

"Didn't St. George come from Cappadocia?"

Natasha ignored me and, instead, turned towards

the entrance. "Come! we go on!" We scattered briefly through the various divisions of this cavernous, barrel-roofed church with its adjoining rooms. The Reverend waited patiently till the last one of us had departed before following after his flock. "You asked about St. George," he remarked kindly. "You're right. In the 'Golden Legend' in the late Middle Ages he is described as a knight from Cappadocia. But in truth little if anything is known about him."

"Perhaps he was one of the monks and lived in one of these caves?" I suggested.

"Who knows? Think of what they must have endured up here. They had no furniture, no comforts, no glass to their windows. Can you imagine what it could have been like in winter?"

I dug around in my bag for a piece of paper, a photocopy of a letter from St. Basil. In it he had described mid-winter in Cappadocia: '...covered over with a blanket of snow, and when you receive it (the letter) and touch it with your hands, you will recognize how cold a thing it is and how it characterizes the sender who lurks within and cannot put his head out of his chamber. For the houses we possess are graves until spring returns and brings us who were corpses back to life, once more bestowing existence upon us, as upon plants.'

"I thought you might be amused by this description from St. Basil's letters," I said.

"Oh, thank yoooo." The Reverend always said 'thank yoooo' in a long drawn out appreciative way which made you feel good.

"Keep it," I said. "I've another copy." We were building up a friendly understanding. Before coming out I had telephoned him and had said I wasn't the most believing person in the world, rather the opposite, and taking communion and all that made me apprehensive. He had assured me that nothing was compulsory, and just to come along and enjoy it. He was so affable, I felt I could confide doubts and receive spiritual help if the right moment came along. Just then we had to hurry after the troope of British Christians who were holding each other's arms to help each other up steep steps, and over high thresholds into yet another cave church. The view along the ravine was of weathered, Hans Christian Anderson fairy-tale creations, the spiritual homes of fanatical minds with haggard bodies.

In one of his letters Basil the Great reproved a 'fallen' monk who had committed adultery. He reminded the monk of how his former devotion to God had been admirable and '...You rid your flesh of all its fat, nobly drained the channels of your abdomen dry, and by compressing your stomach itself with fastings, you caused your outstanding ribs, like the eaves of a house, to cast a shadow about the region of your navel...' I couldn't imagine any woman finding him attractive!

"There just has to be something slightly unhinged about them," I found myself saying aloud. Know-it-all-been-everywhere was standing beside me.

"You think so? I find it rather marvellous."

"I mean, to regard life in this world as something to be scorned is surely an affront to being alive at all?"

"Well, I wouldn't say that. After all it's the soul that's important."

"Up to a point. The soul disciplines the body - well, according to Socrates."

"Socrates? Really?"

"But for God-crazed monks to live like animals to

prove to God they worship and adore him, seems to me insane - and to suppose God will be pleased by it! What does that say about God?"

Know-it-all-been-everywhere regarded me with a tolerant smile. She had already told me one night at dinner that she had 'seen the light' and believed in the 'power of Jesus', but also liked to feel she was broadminded and understanding of those unable to see things as she did.

"Why does God give men bodies if he's so longing for their souls? Why not just grab the souls and have done with it?" I said.

"Dear, oh, dear. Worse and worse!" she remarked calmly.

"Can you hear me at the back?" Natasha's voice carried over the heads of the Close Cropped Christians who were gathered in front of her. "I've been asked about the beliefs the people had before the coming of the Christians here. So far as we know the people worshipped the Mother Goddess about whom I have already spoken. She was Cybele, sometimes pronounced Kybele, and the goddess of fertility. In some of these caves archaeologists have found traces of sacrifice to this goddess. Now, do you have any other questions?"

"Was there no worship of Zeus, or Apollo?" I shouted from the back.

"Then we will move on. Come! Just be careful of the steps down, please!"

When the Moslems finally conquered the area, they built mosques for themselves and left the Christian monks alone in their caves to keep up their bid for salvation. They too had their share of mystics and ascetics but not to the same extreme as the Christians. They were the Sufis, and I had already briefed myself about them because, after

Cappadocia, we were to travel on to Konya, a university town, situated in the heart of Anatolia. It was to Konya that pilgrims came to honour the great Sufi mystic, Jalal al-Din Rumi, better known as Mevlâna. The Whirling Dervishes had originated with the Sufis. To see the Whirling Dervishes was listed as a possibility in the tour's itinerary, and I very much hoped we'd see them.

Prayers were said and then the Reverend called for a period of silence in which to 'offer to God what is in your hearts'. I thought silence was a good thing so that words for once wouldn't interfere or work their sophistry on thoughts and feelings. So we were silent. The silence continued and continued till I wondered if the Reverend had fallen asleep. Silence is quite odd as, after thirty seconds, you wait in expectation for the next thing: a word, some sign of life - sophistry - anything. Strange how life is a constant flow of words, either spoken, heard or read.

We were in the tiny Church of St. Paul, a narrow building squeezed between larger ones in Konya (old Iconium) where St. Paul had come and preached in a Jewish synagogue. Natasha had already enlightened us about a large Jewish community in the area. On the way to Konya the Reverend had read aloud from Acts 14 which described how St. Paul and his companion, Barnabus, had been stoned out of the city. Finding himself in nearby Lystra St. Paul had cured a cripple, and the sight had prompted the people to cry out: '"The gods have come down to us in the likeness of men!"' They believed that the two were Zeus, god supreme of the Greek world, and Hermes, his messenger, which to me proved that the ancient gods (who to early Christian fathers were not gods at all but demons) were able to perform miracles also, and served their purpose perfectly well so far as the spiritual welfare of mortals was concerned.

In this extended silence my mind drifted from the anxiety of the Cappadocian monks about the salvation of their souls, to the ancient Greeks who'd believed that the souls of the dead either went to the Land of the Blessed or, if some outrage had been committed against humanity, went to Tartarus for eternal punishment. I continued to think it rather better to have a number of gods passing judgement on your fate than one almighty angry God.

Silence! Yet words or visions like a documentary film script slid past my mind's eye - odd to have a mind's eye, an eye in ones mind! That afternoon when we'd first arrived in Konya, we'd been taken straight to the major attraction, the Mevlâna Museum, a complex of domes and minarets set in a rose garden with a fountain. My mind's eye had envisaged it quite wrongly so I'd been unprepared for its artistic layout. Certainly the mind's eye had seen the rose garden but had not prepared me for the scent of the damask roses. It was interesting that the mind's eye could visualize but lacked the other human senses. It could foresee but couldn't experience the sensual reality of anything. For that the body was needed; for the scent of roses the nose was required.

Because Konya was at the centre of the Anatolian plateau, placed conveniently at the meeting point of trade routes between east and west, north and south, the Selçuk Moslems had made it their capital. In the thirteenth century the sultan (Sultan Alâeddin Keykubad) established a court of artists and scholars there and it became a renowned centre of literature and learning.

It was in 1228 that Mevlâna's family settled in Konya at the invitation of the sultan. As a Sufi Moslem he sought direct experience of God in this life by purification and discipline of mind and body. Some say the Sufis originated from Moslems influenced by the early Christian ascetics of the Egyptian desert (Egypt fell to the Moslems in 641 A.D.)

In time Mevlâna became renowned for his mysticism and scholarship, both in Greek philosophy and Islamic law, and students flocked to his lectures. His life completely changed, however, when quite unexpectedly he made a new acquaintance and some sort of mental spark ignited. This so overwhelmed Mevlâna with love for the mystic scholar Shams-i-Tabriz, that from then on all else was forgotten. He neglected his pupils and sat closeted with Shams discussing mysticism and philosophy for days, weeks and months.

"That's homosexual love for you!" said Know-it-all-been-everywhere. But I assured her that in the books I'd read about him there'd been no mention of homosexuality, only of the extraordinary spiritual affinity between them.

"Well! The more I travel, the more I discover things that endlessly surprise me!" she remarked.

When Shams disappeared (believed to have been murdered) Mevlâna was so anguished by his loss that he could find no consolation except in an outpouring of devotional poetry. He wrote about the soul's separation from God (or the beloved) and the yearning to bring about a reunion.

'Know that Love's branches are in Eternity-without-beginning, its roots in Eternity-without-end...'

When Mevlâna died, his son and disciples built a

mausoleum for him around which the Mevlâna Museum was constructed. Earlier that afternoon we'd been let loose to wander about there alone. I had gone at once to the Mevlâna tomb situated in a magnificent corner of a large hall. The area around it was decorated with illuminated Arabic calligraphy and Islamic designs in red, gold and black. The sarcophagus was raised on a catafalque and covered in a richly decorated pall at the head of which was Mevlâna's turban wrapped around an elongated crown. Near to him were an array of similar sarcophagi of relatives and disciples, each with the dervish camel's-hair tall cap at the head of it. High above the tomb of Mevlâna rose a conical, fluted dome, a visible landmark to all approaching from the streets outside as its exterior was tiled in a distinctive turquoise.

Mevlâna's most famous words were: 'Come, come again, and again...Come, whether you be unbelievers, idolaters or worship fire...Our hearth is not the threshold of despair. If you have broken your resolve a hundred times, come again...' I found the words refreshingly open-minded and unthreatening; there was no hell-fire and brimstone if one fell short of what was expected, which was a pleasant change.

The Reverend broke the silence at last. "I know we have no musical accompaniment, but I think we can manage hymn number two hundred and sixty-one without it," he said with boyish enthusiasm, regarding the back wall over our heads. He gave us time to find the hymn, then led the singing in an uninhibited way and everyone joined in: 'Bless'd are the pure in heart, / For they shall see our God; / The secret of the Lord is theirs, / Their soul is Christ's abode...'

Two of the Close Cropped Christians broke into a

descant as the rest soldiered on with the familiar tune. I wondered how many of them thought about the words. Harry joined in with the second verse: 'Still to the lowly soul / He doth Himself impart, / And for His dwelling and His Throne / Chooseth the pure in heart...'

I began to wonder why God couldn't impart himself to all and sundry? Mevlâna had spoken of 'naughting the self' in order to find purity of thought. I was, I supposed, on an endless ego trip.

'Lord, we Thy Presence seek; / May ours this blessing be; / Give us a pure and lowly heart, / A temple meet for Thee.'

"Well! I don't have to tell you how well you all did with that!" exclaimed the Reverend with a beaming smile, looking again at the wall beyond our heads.

The little Church of St. Paul was run by two Roman Catholic nuns, one of whom now addressed us in broken English. There was about her a humility which was striking; if ever there was one blessed and pure in heart, it was her. When she could find no English word to tell us about the difficulties she faced in Islamic Konya, she didn't appear uneasy or embarrassed but looked to the Reverend or Natasha for prompting. There were only twenty-five Christians in all Konya, she told us, and it was a struggle to keep their Christian faith alive and continue with their charitable works. I supposed they were financed by the Pope who would want to show the Roman Catholic flag in such unlikely places. The young nun was so gentle, so composed, that we all fell for her. I would have liked to have emulated her, but it would have required a supreme and near impossible task of 'naughting myself'. Anyway, how boring it would be if we were all similarly 'pure in heart' - well, that was what I thought.

Soon we were on the coach and being borne along the streets of Konya to our hotel. Natasha told us 'please to observe' how few Moslem women there were to be seen; that was because Konya was financed by Iran and was, consequently, subjected to Islamic fundamentalist control. "You must please observe the houses, the clean streets, how fine they all appear to the visitor! It is because money is poured in from Iran. But believe me, there is a price the people pay for what you see. They are not free." When she had finished delivering a tirade against Iran, fundamentalism, the problems of women, Turkish democracy or lack of it, the Reverend took the mike and informed us that it was confirmed that the Whirling Dervishes would celebrate their rites before us that evening after dinner. That was really good news.

The Whirling Dervish ceremony (it is never called a 'show' or 'performance' as it is a mystic rite) took place in a large hall in the basement of our hotel. The Sufi whirling dance had first started in Baghdad two hundred years before Mevlâna, but Mevlâna had introduced music and chanting to it which was something quite new to the Moslem world.

I found myself sitting beside a slightly inadequate middle-aged daughter who'd never left home, and whose mother on her other side now leant across to speak to me. She talked happily about the various tours they'd been on. "I always like to be with a group," said Mum, "as I never know what I want to see and it's easier to have others decide for me. Is Harry unwell?" she enquired kindly.

I explained that he'd had a headache and thought he'd

have an early night. I didn't say that as the cost of seeing the Whirling Dervishes was another twenty pounds a head, he'd decided to let me do it alone and to tell him about it afterwards.

The conversation stopped abruptly as there were signs that the ceremony was about to begin. Somebody was sprinkling powder around the polished wooden floor.

"That must be to help the dervishes slide their feet or whatever they do," whispered Mum. "I remember my mother doing that before giving a dance when we were in India - at the time of the Raj, you know."

We settled back on our chairs as the formalities started with the entry of the dervishes (mostly lithe young men with moustaches). They were dressed in black mantles (symbolic of the grave) over white shirts and long white garments (representing the shroud) and their tall camel's-hair caps (which symbolized the tombstone). The Sheikh - each dervish lodge has a Sheikh who is the head - took his stand on a 'pelt' (in this case a red sheepskin) which is the Sufic throne and place of honour. Beside him were two more white sheepskins, though for what reason I didn't know. The Sheikh had a neat white beard and was distinguished from the others by a broad blue-green band around his camel's-hair cap. Beside him was a dervish with a grey beard who must have held some special rank as he remained beside the Sheikh watching proceedings for most of the ceremony. His eyes had a tyrannical, unblinking glint about them, and I thought he looked excessively cruel.

After the dervishes had bowed to the Sheikh they began to circle the hall slowly, one step at a time. I noticed one stifling a yawn which was rather unmystical, but I supposed that repetitive ceremonies in front of tourists turned the mystical into the commercial and could become tedious. At twenty pounds a head it was surely worth whirling to every tour group that came to the hotel?

To become a Mevlevi dervish was a long and arduous business, requiring the novice one thousand and one days of severe trial. First, he had three days of meditation to test his patience, and to see if he was spiritually gifted enough for it. After a further period of isolation, he was then instructed about the internal organization of the Sufi order. Then would come the period of study and the obligation to do numerous boring chores required by the Convent. After the one thousand and one days, if he was assessed as having the right qualities, he could then wear the cap and cloak of the Mevlevi order. If a novice was not considered suitable, then his shoes (which were always left outside his cell at night) would be turned with their toes outward signifying that he must leave. There would be no discussion, just this unspoken peremptory order which he was obliged to obey without question.

There were five seated musicians on the other side of the hall from us. A slight figure with a small beard began to chant, a long liturgical chant which was rather mournful. The Sheikh was standing on his red sheepskin with his second in command beside him. The dervishes next prostrated themselves before him and kissed the ground. Soon small kettle-drums were beaten and the reed flute (said to represent the human voice sorrowing as the soul seeks reunion with the loved one) began its plaintive sound. These were joined by a lute accompaniment.

After a while the dervishes removed their black mantles and, having completed the preliminary formalities, began to pivot slowly, keeping their black slippered feet close to the ground. At this stage they had their arms crossed, hands to their shoulders. Gradually they increased the momentum and stretched out their arms, the right hand palm up to the heavens, the left down to the earth. They spun on their own axis (the art is learned by novices turning around a nail in the floor placed between their toes). As they spun they revolved around the hall which I'd read represented the planets orbiting the sun. They did this in a state of ecstasy, believing that each completed circle brought them to a greater knowledge of the ultimate truth. The word 'whirling' is a misnomer as they never whirled so much as revolved slowly and rhythmically, some with their heads inclined to their shoulders, their eyes semi-closed. On several occasions the second in command walked through the middle of the circle passing glaring messages with his unblinking eyes to any wayward dervish, and watching critically to see how far each was in ecstasy.

Then the Sheikh himself passed through them treading, it is said, the invisible central axis which separates the known world from the eternal. The second in command followed after him and I waited for a collision which would break the monotony and wearisome repetitive revolutions. I had understood that the Sheikh too would whirl but, instead, he and his second in command drew back the right side of their black mantles and inclined their heads, which I supposed symbolized that the heart and ear were open to the mystical revelations. When the Sheikh returned to his pelt the dancing slowly came to an end and, after formally bowing to the Sheikh with arms crossed again, the dervishes put on their black mantles and filed out.

"All that whirling! Oh, dear! I feel quite dizzy - a little sick."

"Oh, Mum!"

"I think you'll have to give me a hand, dear."

"Let me help!" said one of the male Close Cropped Christians.

"I'll be better in a minute or two. A little air, perhaps."

She left, an erect and dignified figure, supported on either side by helping hands. As the others drifted out chattering together, I sat on quietly thinking about what I'd seen.

During his lifetime Mevlâna had no idea that his memory would live on; he himself was too busy enlightening his disciples, and coming to terms with his own tragedies, to think about what would happen to the world after his death. Like Christ he had probably never given a thought to the long term consequence of his mortal existence. Would Christ have thought that two thousand years on people calling themselves Christian would be attending churches and listening to his teachings? Did Mevlâna wonder whether the dervishes would be whirling in the next century, or in the next millennium, come to that?

Mevlâna had always thought of death as a rebirth into divine love; his own death, he said, would be his 'night of union' with God (and his beloved Shams). There was something profound in his mysticism which I found I could almost relate to. 'God is exceedingly near to you,' he wrote. 'Whatever thought and idea you conceive, God is next to it. For He gives existence to the thought and idea and places it before you. But He is so near that you cannot see Him. What is so strange about that? Whatever you do, your intellect is with you, initiating the action. But you cannot see the intellect. Although you see its effects, you cannot see its essence.'

When I'd told Harry about Mevlâna saying that God was so near to you you couldn't see him, Harry had replied: "Well, there you are, then! No need to worry any more!"

I noticed suddenly that everyone around me had gone and reluctantly I followed after them. As I left the hall, I saw several young men emerging from another door with refreshments and sitting themselves around a table. I recognized them as the dervishes now dressed in jeans with open neck shirts. I couldn't resist approaching them to tell them how interesting I had found their celebration. Did any of them speak English, I enquired? No, none of them - well, one of them spoke just a little. In sign language I managed to convey my appreciation and asked him if his father had been a dervish? Father no dervish, came the reply. How long had he been a dervish? I counted on my fingers - years, how many? Ah, ten years. The chanter appeared and joined them.

By now I was caught up in the moment and was wanting to learn more about them, but I could only express myself in sign language. I smiled at the chanter and said as best I could how I had found the music and his chanting wonderful; my hands went from my throat to the heavens in an attempt to describe my meaning. For some inexplicable reason this immediately prompted the small bearded dervish to begin chanting again for my benefit. He was only about two feet from me and, as he chanted, he gazed into my eyes. I thought him rather charming as his voice flowed from him, and I noted that his eyes were a pale blue-grey. When he stopped I repeated my charade expressing my admiration whereupon, as though I'd touched a spring in his throat, he began chanting again. I was annoyed that I didn't know a word of Turkish, though what is more international than music? He chanted for a while then stopped, and the other dervishes gathered around me and one of them said 'come!' whereupon I followed them into the hall again. By now the hall was unlit except for the shaft of light which came through the open door. There the vocalist held me in his gaze and started chanting yet again. I remembered the words of Mevlâna: 'Come, come again, and again... Come, whether you be unbelievers, idolaters or worship fire... Our hearth is not the threshold of despair. If you have broken your resolve a hundred times, come again...'

I didn't know what was in the mind of the chanter or the others, but I knew what was fleetingly in mine. He continued to gaze unwaveringly into my eyes as he sang (what the words were I had no idea: 'Meet me at midnight and we will make love?') How would I know? What I did know was that my situation was weird, slightly ridiculous and, perhaps, increasingly foolish. When he at last stopped, I made no more gestures for fear of setting him off again, thanked him profusely and, smiling and salaaming to all in general, quickly left.

"Where have you been?" asked a Close Cropped Christian.

"With the dervishes," I said.

"Alone?"

"Yes."

"Were you able to commune?"

"Not at all. But the chanter chanted again."

"Really?"

I shrugged it off. "What is the good if you don't understand anything?"

"It's not a question of understanding but seeing the way other people practise their faith, that's what's interesting," said Know-it-all-been-everywhere. "I've seen a lot of weird things in my time which I haven't understood."

The dignified and erect figure of Mum came in from the street, still supported on either side. All attention switched to her. Was she feeling better? "Much better, thank you. All that whirling! I just have to get it out of my mind!"

"I expect you're tired. After all we've been on the go since - well, I don't know about you, but I was awake at six," said Know-it-all-been-everywere kindly.

"Yes, I think I'll go up to bed. We really have had a long day and tomorrow we've another early start. Oh, dear!"

"May I have your attention, please!" cried Natasha when we had all descended from the coach. It was several days later and we were now in Ephesus. We stood beside a marshy area where ducks quacked and wild flowers and grasses grew abundantly. Here and there a column drum lay prostrate amongst the weeds.

"If you look in the direction I am pointing, you will see the only remaining column of the temple of Artemis." She turned towards us, her eyes scanning the forlorn group to check if we were listening. "You may not believe me when I say to you that we are standing where there was formerly the ancient port of Ephesus. Pilgrims coming by sea would have seen this temple as they sailed into the harbour here." She paused to see our reaction, but was probably disappointed as there was a light drizzle and we all stood drooping listlessly. "You have to imagine it!" Pause again - more disappointment. "How can I describe it? I cannot. But with its many columns and its great cult figure it was considered one of the seven wonders of the world!"

We had just come from the main Ephesus site several kilometres away where I'd expected the great temple to be.

There in the ruins of Roman Ephesus the Reverend had stood in the large amphitheatre and read aloud from Acts 19. The rest of us had sat on the tiered stone seats to listen, whilst other tour groups watched curiously. Natasha had stood beside the Reverend seemingly attending to his every word, leaning forward lop-sidedly, weighed down by her heavy shoulder-bag; when listening she always held this posture as though waiting for a starting pistol to be fired.

The Reverend read how rioting had broken out against St. Paul's preaching, because this new Christian religion threatened the livelihoods of those dependent on the worship of Artemis.

"I don't know if I have said this to you earlier, and I am sorry if I repeat myself," rang out Natasha's voice, "but I think what I am about to say to you is important. Before building this temple of Artemis down here I want you all to know that first she had a temple in the hills where the Mother Goddess Kybele, sometimes pronounced Cybele, had earlier also been worshipped by the Anatolians. Artemis was goddess of the wild animals and nature, and the people they see her also as the goddess of fertility, as was the great Mother Goddess Kybele before her and as the Virgin Mary was after her." She searched our faces and saw mostly blank expressions. "Are you attending to me, please!" Natasha was clapping her hands in order to make herself heard above the quacking of ducks and to draw the attention of her group. "I cannot emphasize to you too much that you have here at Ephesus a history of mother goddesses, finishing as we have seen with the holy mother of Jesus Christ. Do you remember the ruins of the Church of the Virgin Mary where we have just been?" She searched our faces and saw mostly blank expressions.

Whilst up at the Ephesus site she'd taken us to the ruins of the fifth century church dedicated to the Virgin Mary. It had been built in her honour because, it was believed, she'd come to Ephesus with St. John who had been asked by Jesus at his crucifixion to take care of his mother.

We were a shivering group in mackintoshes and waterproof hats, some of us holding umbrellas. The day was overcast and at Ephesus we'd had a thunderstorm. I would remember Ephesus, not so much for the city's marble ruins which included the marble temple of the Emperor Domitian who demanded worship as a god, or the stupendous amphitheatre where rioting had broken out against St. Paul, but for the violent splitting-asunder-of-rocks type of thunder, during which Harry and I had sheltered from the rain in an alcove in the ancient marble library of Celsus.

If I wished I were a better sheep amongst the Reverend's flock, Harry in contrast was delighted with being tethered to Britishness, hygiene and being carried everywhere by coach. "Much better than hanging around for a bus," was his comment. "Just enough freedom to lounge and the food is good. No stomach trouble, thank the Lord!" Harry's past journeys were mostly remembered for how he'd fared, not for where he'd been.

"Before we leave here," shrilled Natasha, "I want you all to look up there to where I am pointing. To me it is interesting that you have the three stages of religion here in Anatolia. Here you have the pagan, and up there you can see the early Christian Church of St. John, and a little lower to the left is the 14th century Mosque of Isa Bey built when the Selçuk Moslems conquered the land, giving their name to the town. Now are there any questions?"

I wanted to know if we'd be going up there, but my standing with Natasha was so volatile I'd learned it was best to remain silent. I asked the Reverend later who shook his head. "Sadly no," he replied. I decided that if the opportunity presented itself I would go alone.

"Now, this afternoon we will be driving up into the hills to see what is today a place of pilgrimage approved by the Vatican. It is the House of the Virgin Mary where, they say, she lived until her death under the care of the apostle John."

The Reverend asked for a moment of our attention. "Some of you might like to read John 19. 25-26 where Jesus commends his mother to John's care at his crucifixion. Now, I am sure you will all be glad to hear I have asked, and received permission, to hold a service of Holy Communion in the small chapel up there. I think you will agree this is a singular privilege, giving us an opportunity for quiet reflection in a unique and holy place sanctified by the Vatican." The Reverend looked across to Natasha to indicate he had finished.

"Thank you for that," Natasha said. Her behaviour towards the Reverend was always cordial, even ingratiating. She now clapped her hands again. "Come! We go now to have our lunch and to get ourselves warm!" She led the way back to the coach, walking with quick steps and leading with one shoulder, the other hauling the heavy shoulder-bag like a snail's shell on her back. Soon the Reverend was standing by the driver doing his counting-the-flock act, using his index finger and silently mouthing the numbers as he pointed from seat to seat, beginning from the back and coming forward, to make sure we were all on board.

Dripping plane trees made our arrival at Meryemana gloomy. The House of the Virgin Mary which we entered had been turned into a chapel with an altar; behind the altar stood a bronze statue of the Virgin. There was a flagged floor and the stone walls were bare except for a few holy pictures. Numerous candles of supplication flickered. Harry said in a loud whisper: "What's the history of the place?" Whereupon one of the Close Cropped Christians went 'Shhhh!' in a loud hiss and pointed to a notice saying 'Silence'.

Outside I told Harry what little I knew. Apparently, a bed-ridden German nun had had repeated visions of the exact location where the Virgin Mary had spent her last days. When she'd reported it to the appropriate ecclesiastical authorities, an archaeological dig had been organized and the foundations of this first century house had come to light. "She'd never been out of Germany and yet could pin-point the site on a map," I told Harry. "The Pope then came here in 1967, and it was finally approved by the Vatican as a place of pilgrimage."

A shiningly serene-faced nun in a pale blue habit flitted past us, and I saw the Reverend draw her aside for a few words. Soon he was beckoning and summoning us for the service. We trooped into another chapel and sat on benches. The Reverend disappeared and returned, a cherubic figure in white and gold vestments.

The sceptic in me tried to atune itself to the occasion but with little success. Natasha sat in front and I was surprised to see her joining in the responses.

"'We do not presume to come to this your table, merciful Lord, trusting in our own righteousness, but in your manifold and great mercies...'" the Reverend intoned, and I noticed Natasha was listening attentively.

If I was sometimes at odds with Natasha, I at least admired her attitude to religion. When the Reverend had been taking a Communion Service several days earlier in the ancient ruins of a church, we had all been standing in a semi-circle and I'd noticed then that she had had no qualms about eating the sacramental bread and drinking from the chalice. Later, I'd braved her wrath and asked her about it, and for once she'd replied to my question: "I was born a Moslem but to me all religions are the same. When I am with Christians, I do what Christians do; when in a pagan sanctuary, then I am pagan; and when in a mosque, I am Moslem. I never have any problem with it!" I was impressed by her lack of scruple.

The Reverend's voice was continuing, using the lower tonal register which priests tend to use as they lead up to the climax of Holy Communion. "'Grant us therefore, gracious Lord, so to eat the flesh of your dear Son Jesus Christ and to drink his blood...'" I didn't at all want to drink the blood of Christ or eat his body, and wondered if it was a continuation of the pagan habit of gaining strength by devouring the flesh of live bulls, which was a part of the ritual worship of Dionysos, god of wine.

Perhaps, sensing something was amiss amongst his communicants, the Reverend gently said that if any of us didn't want to take the sacraments, to hold our hands down. The blessing which I received instead came as a surprising balm.

After the service, we followed Natasha down the various terraces to the holy spring. Being not entirely without holy belief of some sort, I'd brought a small container to take away some water which was said to work miracles. But the holy spring came out of taps plumbed for the purpose along a stone wall. There didn't seem to be anything holy about it and the earlier blessing, which had been like a balm, blew away leaving me a rebel again. Beyond the line of taps the wall was smothered with votive offerings.

"You have to understand that it is not only Christians who come here to petition the Virgin Mary," said Natasha in a hushed pianissimo, loud enough to be heard but not so loud as to disturb other pilgrims. "Do you know that Jesus is a great prophet in Islam? This makes his mother Mary of much importance to Moslems. It is for this reason that here it is a place of pilgrimage for Moslems who also believe in the healing powers of the Virgin Mary."

"May we take some of the water?" asked one of the Close Cropped Christians.

"Yes, of course!"

Several from our group filled various small containers with the holy water. Natasha continued in her stage whisper: "Maybe you are not aware that the villagers of Sirince where tomorrow we go, came every year to this place for the Orthodox summer festival. This, it is thought, may be a continuation of the earlier summer pagan festival. They came to the Panagia Kapoulu or Kapili (the All Holy Gateway). There are several pronunciations, though I like to think that the All Holy Kapili is a variant spelling of Kybele, the Anatolian Mother Goddess."

"What's the Orthodox summer festival?" Harry asked me as the group began to drift away.

"It must be the Virgin Mary's Assumption held on the 15th August," I replied.

"And what's Assumption?"

"Her being taken up to heaven body and soul," I replied. "You'd say, of course, that the Assumption must be true because the Pope says it is."

"Not necessarily. Yes. No. Well, I don't know."

"What are you two debating?" asked Know-it-all-been-everywhere, coming alongside us.

"The Assumption of the Virgin Mary," I said.

"What about it?"

"It's an odd sort of idea."

"I think Pope Pius XII defined the doctrine finally not so long ago."

"Oh? When was that?"

"Well, he died in 1958."

"Good heavens! Quite recently. How odd."

"Why odd? When I was in Rome I met the Pope - well, not exactly met, but I saw him. A fabulous man. Very moving."

As we walked back to the coach I found myself alone with the Reverend and confessed to him that I'd been wrestling with demons during the Communion Service. I hadn't wanted to take the sacraments because I hadn't felt myself repentant or meek enough.

"Oh, don't let it worry you, my dear," he replied. "It is God working through you."

God working through me? How nice. The Reverend was so calm and kindly, he left me feeling I wasn't a total Christian drop-out, but acceptable for what I was. The balm of my former blessing - which had blown apart in rebellion at seeing taps for holy water - resettled soothingly on my head.

Natasha cast an unsmiling glance in my direction as the Reverend had a word in her ear.

"If she can find her way back to the hotel then there is no problem," I heard her say. The Reverend came down the coach to my seat and told me I would be put down in the town if I still wanted to see Selçuk. I was elated. We were on our way back from visiting the old Greek village of Sirince and were passing through Selçuk. As the visit to Sirince had been an optional extra and Harry could see no point in spending money to see a Greek village in Turkey when he'd seen more than enough in Greece itself, he'd opted out of the trip in favour of an afternoon beside the hotel swimming-pool.

The coach drew up in the centre of town and Natasha pointed me in the direction I should go. She waved an arm - I wasn't sure towards what - and told me that that was where I should get the bus back, or a dolmus. I didn't know what a dolmus was, but got out and felt much as a sheep might feel at having at last got through the hedge to freedom.

The sky was blue and the sun shone. After walking in the direction I'd been told, I enquired of someone where the Church of St. John was and was pointed in the opposite direction to the one Natasha had said - the rat! I passed a Tourist Information Office and double checked before continuing. Eventually I arrived.

The ruins of the church stood on a hill with views to the far distance. Formerly built by the Emperor Justinian in the sixth century, it had been constructed over an earlier church destroyed by earthquake and, under Islam, was converted to a mosque which was also destroyed by earthquake. So many places of worship destroyed in this manner! Perhaps the old Olympians were at war with the Almighty who had, after all, usurped their supremacy?

Recent excavations revealed some of the old church walls. I found the newly renovated tomb of St. John, a white marble-slabbed area with an inscription, flanked at the four corners by small twisted pillars. On a higher elevation were the ramparts to a Byzantine castle.

Apparently, St. John's Jewish-Christian monotheism had so angered the Emperor Domitian that he'd tried to kill him with poison. St. John had drunk the lethal substance but had remained unaffected. Enraged that the poison had failed, the emperor gave it to someone else who died instantly, which clearly proved St. John had some sort of immunity through his faith in God. Enraged even more, the Emperor banished him to the small island of Patmos in the Aegean. Legend has it that he escaped from Patmos floating on a cork.

Before this wonder, however, St. John remained on Patmos for some years where he wrote Revelation, the last book of the New Testament. In it were dire threats to anyone - and especially to Roman emperors - who didn't turn to God and Christ. Interestingly on Patmos, like at Ephesus, there had also been a great temple of Artemis, the site of which is now a monastery dedicated to St. John.

Miracles performed by St. John were numerous and were the main trigger for bringing pagans tumbling into the Christian camp. St. John was adept at performing them and, in the Acts of John in the Apocryphal New Testament (early Christian books not included in the New Testament), there were some striking ones. One such was when one night at Ephesus, St. John was overheard by his companions to cry out: "'I say unto you, O bugs, behave yourselves, one and all, and leave your abode for this night and remain quiet in one place, and keep your distance from the servants of God.'" The next morning at dawn his companions saw a number of bugs standing outside the door where St. John was sleeping. When he finally woke, he praised them for their obedience. Not until he had left the room were they seen running back to enjoy the comforts of his bed again.

Another somewhat more serious story described how St. John one day was met by the Roman praetor who beseeched him to cure his dying wife. On arriving at his wife's bedside, the praetor found she'd already died and was so distraught that he himself fell down dead on top of her.

As can be expected, after much beseeching of God and crying out how there would be very many conversions if he could get them both back to life, St. John called on the wife to arise. Sure enough she 'arose' but, on hearing that her husband had died of grief, she all but expired again and needed all the counselling St. John could give her to keep her from doing just that. He commanded the poor wife to keep faith, though he could see how she was 'shrieking her soul out in silence'. With much praying and extraordinary faith himself, St. John called on God to raise the husband and the story ended happily. Such is the stuff of miracles and with it came conversions.

I sat beside a ruined wall near to a huge bulbous terracotta pot overflowing with wild flowers, and wondered how Harry was enjoying his free afternoon beside the hotel pool. He was immovably entrenched in his own comfortable not-thinking-too-much-about-it beliefs, accepting on trust all that was spooned out by the Church. "Just believe the Church knows what its talking about and stop asking questions," he advised.

"For heaven's sake," I'd found myself saying one day, "if you can't ask questions because the answers are so peculiar, what sort of Alice in Wonderland thinking is that?"

"It's because the answers are unbelievable that you have to NOT ask questions," Harry replied reasonably.

"I'll just have to remain an atheist, then. It's the only solution."

"If that's what you want, why not?" he remarked easily.

I preferred to have a punch-ball to spar with, and Harry was taking it away, leaving me to pick a fight with thin air.

I thought how amazing some of the over eighties in our group were, many of them belonging to what I called the Close Cropped Christian brigade. They were always willing to face a challenge, never daunted by some of the steep and rocky slopes that had to be got up, but would take each other's arm and hobble slowly along. Extraordinarily, they were never tired, and never late for anything. When Harry and I tried to be early for a meal, they were earlier; or to be on time for the coach leaving at eight in the morning, they were already in their seats. I could only suppose their Christianity charged them with endless capabilities despite their apparent frailty. I made a mental note that in old age Christianity might be a useful aid like a crutch or an essential vitamin pill.

I began idly ruminating about the Greek village of Sirince which we'd just come down from. We'd been driven up a mountain along the side of a valley where the vegetation had spectacularly changed from arid to lush vineyards, and small holdings of well tended vegetables, and orchards of citrus and other fruit.

Natasha had stood facing us, swaying perilously and

clinging to the back of a seat as the coach had manoeuvred the bends. The ice-cream cone of a microphone had moved with her as she'd expounded on the historical background of the once Greek village. It had been inhabited by the Greeks following the Trojan War, she'd said - at last she'd admitted the ancient Greeks had come to Anatolia! She'd told us how in 1922 after the First World War, when the Ottoman Empire had been replaced by the modern Republic of Turkey, an exchange of Greeks and Turks had taken place, and the Greeks from Sirince had been forcibly returned to mainland Greece. The Foreign Office had arranged for this exchange and a hundred and fifty thousand Anatolian Greeks had left. What she didn't mention was the terror, murder and mayhem that had taken place with this expulsion. She informed us that, as they'd left the village, the Greeks had set fire to everything. I'd actually read that it had been the Turks who'd incinerated the countryside in order to drive out the Greeks. It was strange how the lush productive small holdings and richly foliaged trees along the valley, put a gloss over any past atrocities that had occurred in the area.

Moslems driving out Christians? Torture, starvation, arson? Forget it! Human beings at peace don't want to remember their past despicable actions. Murder and mayhem belong to the history books, and these can be rewritten for the benefit of whoever has the authority and power to get away with it. Truths get lost in the telling of tales and, whilst there is peace, the evil sub-human elements in mankind lie dormant, or get buried under a mountain of lies.

The village of Sirince itself consisted of terracotta roofed houses with cobbled alleyways ascending the hillside. At its centre was a wide pedestrian thoroughfare in which were stalls and small shops, the whole covered by a woven awning against sun or rain. We'd all followed Natasha in a troupe to this market, with the Reverend taking up the rear like a sheep-dog. We'd been told we could wander around at our leisure and I'd begun to explore a little and watch the village scenes: a peasant riding a donkey down a narrow cobbled alleyway scattering some chickens as he advanced; an old man with a stick walking slowly up between the overhanging houses; the chug-chug of an engine as an old motorbike with side-car came slowly round a corner, ridden by a villager with a bundle behind which turned out to be his wife; she'd had an arm out to a bulging sack balanced on top of brushwood which had been loaded into the side-car. It had passed by and chug-chugged up another narrow alleyway between dilapidated looking houses.

One of the stall holders, a pretty young Turkish girl, had suddenly enquired: "You like antique house? I have house four hundred year old. You like you see?"

"Well - "

Harry had issued me with strict instructions not to stray away from the group, but this was an opportunity too good to be missed.

"Come, I show you. Please, you come."

We'd gone down cobbled alleyways to the edge of the village where we'd had to jump several muddy ditches before arriving at a small courtyard with a tree and a tiny whitewashed house. At the entrance had stood Grandmama wearing flowery Turkish pantaloons, a waistcoat over a white shirt and a patterned head scarf. I'd noticed that a kettle was already boiling on a gas-ring as I was led into a small room in which was a blue painted, free standing staircase with dangerously uneven steps. I was invited to go up which I did cautiously, avoiding a loose tread. There seemed to be only one small whitewashed room with two long rug-covered divans, a table and a single picture on the wall. A small window looked out on to a few trees at the back.

As we'd sat upstairs I'd noticed that the picture on the wall was of the Virgin Mary, and I'd drawn her attention to it. She spoke little English but, putting her hands together, had indicated prayer and wonderment.

I'd said: "Meryemana?"

Eagerly she'd replied: "Yes! Meryemana!"

There in the 'antique house' the young Turkish girl had explained the reason for the picture of the Virgin Mary.

"My mother - "

"Mother - of you?"

"No, no. Mother of mother. Downstair - you meet."

"Grandmother?"

"Yes. She goes with her feet. Walk - she pray. Eight year no children - Now five."

"A miracle!" I'd said.

"Yes, a miracle," she'd agreed.

"And you all live here?" I'd asked her in surprise.

She'd laughed. "Me, husband. Near here house. Husband - my husband, me and baby - other house."

After a while Grandmama had called and we'd gone down the perilous stairs. I'd smiled at her and said the magic word 'Meryemana', to which Grandmama had beamed and made expressive gestures of enlarging her pantaloons with great satisfaction.

We'd sat in the courtyard and drunk apple-tea, and they'd proudly shown me their lace work, spreading item by item out on the clean, newly swept courtyard: table-cloths of all shapes and sizes, napkins, table mats, dressing-table runners and bedcovers. After I'd bought several items, the girl had accompanied me back to the main cobbled and covered market where her family had their stall. Clearly I'd been part of a well contrived sales technique, but I had no regrets.

"So where did you get to?" one of the Close Cropped Christians had demanded, when I'd eventually tracked them down. "We wondered where you'd gone. We waited fifteen minutes for you before deciding to move on." The remark had been accusing.

I'd apologized to the Reverend. "Not to worry!" he'd said kindly. "The main thing is that you've found us." I'd then bought him a bottle of the local wine as a peace offering.

"Oh, thank yoooo," he'd said with evident pleasure. "Thank yoooo so much!"

Now at Selçuk I left the ruins of the Church of St. John and went on down the road, visiting on the way the Isa Bey Camii, a mosque built in 1375 A.D., which had in its construction some columns from the temple of Artemis. A little way further the land dipped down and extended in a marshy expanse to where, in the distance, stood the single column marking the site of the original temple.

A further miracle of St. John is related in the Acts of John. It describes how one day he had gone to the temple of Artemis where crowds had gathered for her annual festival. Everyone was dressed in white except for John who chose to make himself conspicuous in black. He climbed onto a rostrum and called out to the people, telling them that if Artemis was truly a powerful goddess then let him die there and then; but if his own God was more powerful, then let him slay all of them. As they had already witnessed various miracles they were wary of the power of John's God. Sure enough, after John did a lot of praying, '...the altar of Artemis was parted into many pieces... And the half of the temple fell down, so that the priest was slain at one blow...' And all the people were horrified and amazed and fell on their faces and then, getting up, cried out: "'The God of John only do we know, and him hereafter do we worship, since he hath had mercy upon us!'" In due course the corpse of the dead priest was brought to John, and he was asked to raise him from the dead. John told the man to raise him himself, and told him to say: "'John the servant of God saith to thee, Arise.'" And the young man did what he was told and, sure enough, the priest came to life and became a Christian, as did everyone else who saw these marvels.

Well! It's hardly surprising under those circumstances that Christianity spread. Perhaps the surprising thing is it took centuries.

I took one last look at the remaining column of the temple of Artemis - Artemis, who'd been worshipped in the hills before she'd moved down to Ephesus; who had taken over the sacred sites of the great Mother Goddess Kybele and who was herself replaced by the Virgin Mary, the mother figure to whom people now turn for their ailments and fertility problems.

There was, however, yet another mother goddess who, although not so well known, was believed to have come from Anatolia. She was the mother of Artemis and Apollo. The next day the itinerary included a visit to the ancient oracle site of Apollo at Didyma, home of Apollo's mother Leto. I was curiously excited at the prospect of seeing this pagan site. What Apollo had to say about Christianity and the Jewish God was surprising.

"If you all look now you will see - " We all looked from the coach window expecting something spectacular. "Ah, there it is!" There was what? "Did you see it? That was the ancient Sacred Way from Miletus to Didyma!"

For a split second I had seen a weedy, paved track. We were on our way to the last of three pagan sanctuaries that day, to the great sanctuary and oracle of Apollo at Didyma. I was by now bog-eyed with ruins and awash with Natasha's flow of words.

For me Didyma was one of the highlights of this journey. Didyma had been famed throughout the ancient world for its oracle of Apollo and came second in importance to Delphi. As an oracle it had been approached on the question of God and Christ, and how the pagan gods stood in relation to the God of the Jews. All fascinating stuff and taken up with gusto by early Christian writers who were bent on belittling paganism and advancing Christianity.

There were at the time many Jewish communities in Anatolia and the idea, from Plato in the fifth century B.C. onwards, that there was one supreme deity over and above the others, was widespread. This higher god was sometimes identified with Zeus but was also considered nameless and, therefore, identifiable with the God of the Jews.

One of the questions put to Apollo at Didyma was whether Jesus was God or man. The response had been: 'He was mortal in flesh, wise in miraculous works, but convicted by Chaldaean judges he was nailed to stakes and reached a bitter end.' An early Christian named Lactantius, who'd lived in the third century, quoted this and, with

Christian cunning, argued that since Apollo was a demon not a god then, by saying Christ had been 'mortal in the flesh', he had obviously implied that he was God in spirit.

On the great terrace at Didyma with its three remaining colossal fluted columns and their beautifully decorated column drums, Natasha said: "Now as I know some of you - " her eye singled me out, "would like time to wander at leisure, I suggest we meet at the entrance in half an hour. Does this suit you all?"

With my chains cut I flew down one of the narrow vaulted corridors to the holy adyton (the inner sanctum of Apollo) on a lower level. There, there was a round ancient stone well overgrown with weeds and grasses. The well had been the source of the holy water over which the prophetess had sat, and where she'd received the words of the god.

I tried to visualize the scene of the ancient ritual as I stood beside the well. The prophetess, it was believed, prepared herself for her role by fasting and cleansing herself in the waters of this spring, in this manner opening herself up to the divine light and inspiration of Apollo. A high priest officiated and received the written questions to be put to the god. Only he heard the answers spoken by the prophetess seated over the sacred spring and, from the top of a flight of steps beyond, he would then proclaim them to the gathering.

One of the questions put to the oracle had been concerning the immortality of the soul: Did it survive after death or vanish? The answer was: 'As long as the soul is bound by chains to the body, it meets corrupting experiences and yields to mortal ills. But when it finds quick mortal release after the body's decay, it goes entirely to the sky, being ever ageless, and remains forever incorruptible. For this is what the first-born divine providence ordained.'

This area had been converted to a Christian church in the fifth or sixth century and it had been the seat of a bishop. In the tenth century it had been destroyed by an earthquake - yet another one knocked down.

I thought about the beautiful Leto, a Titaness (a race of immortals begotten by Heaven and Earth). She was the mother of Apollo and Artemis, and was believed to have come from Didyma. When Zeus had first set eyes on her he'd had one of his almighty love affairs and she'd become pregnant with the divine twins, Apollo and Artemis. As a result, people had sacrificed here at this site not only to Apollo but also to Artemis, Zeus and Leto. Thanks to this immortal romance Leto had also become a mother goddess figure, though soon to be eclipsed by her more illustrious daughter, Artemis.

"How's it going?" enquired Know-it-all-been-everywhere as she ambled by leaning on a walking stick. "Alexander the Great yet again! It's thanks to his patronage that this place revived after the Persians. Extraordinary man!"

What she said was true. Alexander had swept down through Anatolia (in the fourth century B.C.) and the Anatolians had welcomed him as a liberator because, at that time they'd been under the tyrannical Persian yoke. Alexander had poured money into the cities and had reinstated democracy. His policy of freedom and equality amongst men whatever their creed or colour of their skin, had won him great popularity. His mentor had been Aristotle, no less.

"When I was in Egypt," Know-it-all-been-everywhere was saying, "I went to the Siwa Oasis where there's a temple of Zeus Ammun. You'd like it there, I know.

There Alexander was welcomed by the high priest as Son of God. Interesting! Funny thing nobody knows where he was buried - rather like the Virgin Mary, I'm thinking - just disappeared off the face of the earth. Sorry! You're wanting to be alone. We'll speak anon." And she ambled off, determined to make the most of sight-seeing whilst the opportunity was there.

The Reverend strolled towards me, pausing every now and then to read something he had his index finger on in an open book. "They say this was called Ieronda by the Greeks, meaning the 'Holy Place'. All that's gone now with the Turkish Republic. Have you enjoyed the trip?" he enquired kindly.

"Very much."

"We try to keep a balance between organized tours and leaving you free to do your own thing," he went on, without any suggestion of wagging a finger at me. "I was just reading about Roman patronage here. The Roman emperors were keen to keep this place going. You can imagine what fun they had with oracle pronouncements! The Emperor Diocletian, for example, claimed Apollo told him to go ahead and persecute the Christians!"

Harry appeared suddenly, having strode ten times around the temenos for exercise. "Are there you are! Natasha's wanting us to forgather at the entrance near to the Medusa's head."

"We're coming." And the Reverend extended an arm to guide his lost sheep back into the fold. Soon we were back on the bus, and he was doing his counting-the-flock act before making an announcement. That evening, he told us, there would be a prayer meeting at six thirty, followed by a general meeting in which he would give us final instructions for the following day and our flight home.

'...For thine is the kingdom, the power and the glory, for ever and ever, Amen.' The Reverend laid his prayer-book down on the table and allowed a suitable moment to pass before raising his head to give us his final address. We were all standing in a semicircle around a small conference room in our hotel.

"I want to thank yoooo all," he began, "to thank yoooo all for being such good members of this fellowship journey. We have been on a pilgrimage together which has certainly enriched me, as I hope it has you too. And an especial thank yoooooo to our invaluable and able guide Natasha. Thank yoooo, my dear." Bows and smiles in her direction, to which Natasha told us what a privilege it had been for her to take us around her beloved country, and what an exceptionally intelligent lot we'd been. And she herself felt we all owed a special thank you to the Reverend. Whereupon one of the Close Cropped Christians started clapping and we all joined in with enthusiasm. This in itself received another 'Thank yoooooo!' and 'Bless you all for your magnificent contribution to the success of this prayerful journey'.

That evening, despite the many blessings given, despite the example of tolerance and goodwill set by the Reverend, I continued to be an atheist.

Next stop Egypt!

Perhaps I would find enlightenment there...

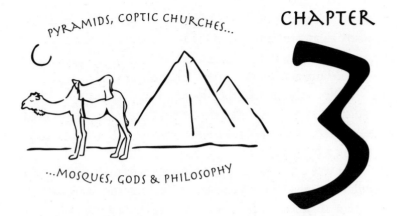

CAIRO & ALEXANDRIA

"What side of the road do they drive on here?" I asked as we left Cairo airport and joined the crush of cars. I was merely curious.

"Good question!" muttered the military voice of our travelling companion. There was only one other couple on this tour, a husband and wife in their sixties whom we'd only just met and liked on sight. He had an air of defiant good humour, passing remarks with a contented take-it-or-leave-it bonhomie. She had wild grey hair and a placid face with watchful eyes.

Lorries, trucks, cars all hurtled along avoiding the odd donkey and cart which had its right of passage amongst the speeding vehicles. There seemed to be no traffic lights and few cars with headlights or even sidelights. Our driver jammed on the brakes of our minibus as a small boy in his night-shirt was hustled through the traffic by his mother in black Arab dress and yashmak.

"Are there many accidents?" I asked Ali, our young tour guide who'd met us at the airport. He was seated in the front seat, one arm over it as he turned towards us, ready to answer any questions.

"Excuse me?"

"Many accidents - smash - bang?" I asked.

"No. The people they look always." He spoke a few words in Arabic with the driver who smiled as he swerved sharply to avoid a youth with several pillion passengers riding a bicycle.

It was ten o'clock at night and neon lights winked from tall buildings, their façades concealing the back streets where dilapidated houses could be briefly glimpsed. The occasional domed mosque with its minarets silhouetted against the night sky flashed by. A youth on a donkey galloped down the central reservation. What fun! There was a life and spirit to the city, a total absence of rules and regulations; there were no visible police.

"The Nile!" declared the military voice.

"No. It is not yet," Ali said. He had an olive complexion and a quiet optimistic manner; his face was not unlike the young Tutankhamun but without the Pharaohnic head-dress. I was rapidly falling in love with Cairo with its hurly-burly bustle, and joyful free-for-all on the roads. Instead of crash-helmets motorcyclists wore tarbushes (close fitting embroidered caps); instead of speed limits and road cameras to impose fines, there was a cheerful thrust and go, each driver fully concentrated on avoiding and being avoided. I said my usual silent prayer to the Almighty for a safe journey and added my apologies for not believing in him.

We'd left Gatwick early that morning and had flown first to Luxor. The 9/11 atrocities six months back had put the world on high alert. Moslem fundamentalists had shown America that to support Israel and to be a high-tech weapons super-power, able to kill thousands at the touch of a button, could be equalled by knife-wielding Moslem suicide-bombers, hijacking airliners and targeting buildings. The name Osama bin Laden had suddenly become headline news. When I found I could read his name in Arabic I felt remarkably pleased with my progress in the language.

From Luxor we'd flown on to Cairo. As we'd assembled to be led out to a small eighteen-seater plane, a large Egyptian in white turban and brown robe with several black clad wives whose bodies looked packed with high explosives, had tried to join us, but he'd been firmly turned away by armed police. I was learning that being guided around Egypt was a serious security matter.

Harry nudged me. "Is that a pyramid?" he asked. He didn't want to get excited about something that might be something else.

Our military companion spotted it. "Pyramid!" he yelled.

Under subtle flood-lighting the great Giza pyramid and its two companions towered mysteriously in their desert setting, soaring from their massive circumferences to their triangular points against the night sky.

"Tomorrow you go there," said Ali. "Afterwards you see the Archaeological Museum."

I leaned forward to Ali. "Is it possible," I asked, "for me to go to the Coptic quarter instead of the museum?"

Fearful that I was rocking the smooth running of this tour, Harry quickly said: "Of course you can't!" Ali eyed me quietly.

"I particularly want to see it," I persisted.

"I find out for you," said Ali calmly.

"And - if it's possible, the El Amr Mosque and the

Mosque of El Husayn?" If I was to stick my neck out I might as well stretch it as far as I could.

Far from looking troubled Ali had an air of quiet pride that anyone could be interested in early mosques; it was a new experience for him. "I tell the guide tomorrow and he will help you if he can," he said.

We never discovered our retired-from-the-army companion's rank but Harry and I privately referred to him as the Brig. His wife asked me what Coptic was.

"The Christian Church in Egypt," I told her.

"Oh, do they have a Church in Egypt?" she asked in a charmingly vague manner.

We arrived at the hotel where security police immediately swarmed from a Green (as opposed to a Black) Maria. No doubt they were hoping for some excitement to enliven the end of a long uneventful day. We were politely passed through the hotel security system and we all bleeped alarmingly, but nobody seemed worried. Once in the highly polished foyer of this four star hotel we were welcomed with glasses of tropical fruit juice.

After weeks of planning, days of agitation, and sixteen hours of travel, we'd finally arrived.

The weather in early March was pleasantly warm. Next morning from our hotel bedroom I watched the traffic outside honking and circling a nearby roundabout at speed. Palm trees partially hid the rising hills of the desert beyond. Towering majestically from the gilding of desert sand and veiled in an early morning haze against the sky, were the solid honey-coloured pyramids.

Talk of vision and faith! There before me was the consequence of a Pharaoh who'd had no notion of the Old Testament or Christian God but who had, nevertheless, been moved by an inner spirit to leave something to posterity in order to ensure his own safe passage to the after-life. The sight was unique and eternal; a reminder that the human mind was incalculable, having the ability to envisage and to create an inanimate object which reflected, as though in a mirror, both life and eternity.

Two hours later we were on our way there.

I didn't expect to feel awe at seeing what I'd seen a hundred times in pictures. But to stand close to the Great Pyramid at Giza was, in fact, a profound occasion. It wasn't just its magnificence, but life around it - Arabs in white turbans riding camels with their colourful saddles and harnesses; a mounted armed policeman wearing a peaked cap, navy jacket and white breeches, his portly figure curved to the rhythmic plod, plod of his beast; a pick-up truck containing a delighted family of black garbed women, a rabble of children and their men folk, who'd come out for the day. In fact, most visitors there were Egyptian, there were not many foreign tour groups.

After life, resurrection! The Pharaoh was regarded as the mediator between his people and the gods. Whilst alive he was seen as the manifestation of the god Horus, son of the supreme Osiris and the goddess Isis - a divine triad. On his death it was believed the Pharaoh was transformed into Osiris and the new Pharaoh in his turn became the god Horus.

There had been several Egyptian god triads, mostly associated with different districts of Egypt. The Osiris divine family, however, was widespread. I was particularly interested because the Holy Family of Christianity had been a triad and had fled from Palestine to Egypt (according to St. Matthew's gospel) to escape King Herod's order for all male infants under two to be slaughtered in and around Bethlehem. Joseph had been warned in a dream to escape with his family to Egypt. Come to think of it, they could well have seen the pyramids which would then have been about two and a half thousand years old. That was an astonishing thought.

Naguib, another tour guide for that day, a handsome, scholarly looking young man in spectacles, pointed to the lime-coated apex of the pyramid and informed us that in its heyday the whole pyramid had been covered in lime and highly polished so that it had gleamed in the sunlight.

"Who built the ruddy thing?" demanded the Brig, as much to himself as to anyone, "A battalion of slaves, I suppose?"

Naguib overheard and explained how it had been built in stages by the peasants during the time of the Nile floods when they hadn't been able to work the land. This annual inundation of the Nile had brought rich deposits which had fertilized the soil, leaving it ready for the next sowing. Because the people had regarded the king as a god, so they had served him in order to ensure their good harvests. They had seen everything as a continuous cycle of death, resurrection and life.

"Couldn't the chap reach eternal life with just a few stones marking his grave?" the Brig enquired.

Naguib smiled briefly at the Brig's unanswerable question, before continuing with his information: "On his death, before the Pharaoh can become one with Osiris, he has first to be judged. His heart, which is his true self, must be weighed against the feather of the goddess Maat. She is the goddess of truth, justice and the harmony of the universe. You will find many hieroglyphs showing the weighing of the heart."

"So they also had a Day of Judgement?" I queried.

"Of course." Naguib went on to explain the custom of mummifying the Pharaoh's body and surrounding him with his most valued possessions. It was because on his death his ka (his creative life force) was expected to live on, together with other spiritual aspects of his body. "It is important that his ka is reunited with his ba, which is his personality," continued Naguib. "It is more easy for his ka if it can recognize the king's mummified face and the objects important to him during his life," he explained.

"Ba - ka - ha!" the Brig mumbled.

"Darling, let's listen to Naguib!" murmured the Brig's wife.

"All the stones were brought down the Nile and then transported here. There are here two million, three hundred thousand blocks averaging two and a half tons each. Some are as much as fifteen tons..." Naguib's voice trailed on.

A couple of Arabs rode past us on horses. Several touts followed us at a distance with a variety of different wares - postcards, Arab head-dresses, trinkets.

We were taken to the Solar Museum which contained a magnificent solar barque. It was an enormous construction made of cedar wood, with ropes and oars and everything that was required for the deceased king to be transported through the nether world. There was not only belief in the divine triad but also in the sun-god, Ra. The rising sun in the east bringing light and renewed energy was significant, making the east symbolic of life whilst the west symbolized death, the sinking of the sun on its nightly ritual. The god Ra went through a repetitive daily cycle of life and death and life again. So it was with humans who, at death, joined Ra on the eternal treadmill of setting and rising, darkness and light. Regarding human expectations of death and resurrection, what had changed down the millenniums?

Naguib glanced at his watch. It was time to move on to our next destination, the Archaeological Museum.

"No time for crawling about inside the pyramid?" asked the Brig.

"If we are to have time for the Coptic churches we must leave now," explained Naguib smiling patiently.

"Ah, the Coptic churches! Mustn't miss those, or we'll never be forgiven," grunted the Brig, throwing me an accusing but friendly look.

The armed policeman on his camel was still keeping a vigilant eye on the desert. If a grenade was suddenly thrown I wondered what he'd do about it. His camel had an air of boredom - triangular piles of stones were things only humans could possibly regard as a wonder. The camel's expression was one of resigned superiority, a long held tolerance of human idiocy.

"Will we have time for the Coptic Museum after the Coptic churches?" I asked Naguib. It was mid-afternoon and at last we were being driven to the part of Old Cairo I particularly wanted to see.

Naguib smiled sadly and shook his scholarly head. We were driving past a colourful market with stalls of bright materials, fruit and flowers and baskets of pigeons. Donkeys with their burdens were on their way home and ponies drew carts. There was no sign of the filth on the streets of Cairo I'd been warned about, and no disagreeable smells.

I was elated that the Coptic quarter was being included on the itinerary, though regretted having no time for its museum which had rare second century manuscripts of the Gnostic Gospels. Until their discovery in 1945 these texts had lain concealed in a large earthenware pot hidden in one of the many caves which honeycombed a desert mountain near the village of Nag Hammadi in Upper Egypt. There had been the Gospel to the Egyptians, the Apocalypse of Peter, the Gospel of Truth and many others.

"Isn't it extraordinary!" I remarked involuntarily. Then, realizing that something more was expected from me, I went on: "Extraordinary that the New Testament consists of Matthew, Mark, Luke and John when there were other gospels which could as easily have been used instead."

"What amazing colours! Do look!" The Brig's wife was far more interested in a rail of bright kaftans and scarves. "And terracotta pots! I like those!" she said, turning in her seat to look as we drove past.

"We're not going home carrying terracotta pots!" her husband said. He turned to me: "So what about those gospels?" he demanded, showing sudden interest.

"Oh - well, there were a whole lot of them with quite different versions of the life of Jesus. For example, the Apocalypse of Peter had Peter speaking to Jesus at his crucifixion and asking him if it was really his body being nailed to the cross because he could at the same time see him 'glad and laughing' above it. Jesus replied that he was 'glad and laughing' because only his body was on the cross and he was above as the living Jesus."

"Can't have that!" grumbled the Brig.

"Oh, look! More kaftans!" cried the Brig's wife.

"Drive on! Drive on!" ordered the Brig. "Take you to Brixton market one day, old girl. There you'll find all the kaftans you want."

At the Coptic Museum I'd also wanted to see a crucifix depicting Christ with the god Horus accoutrements, such as a hawk and sun disc on his head. The head-dress marked the transition between pagan thought and Christianity. Horus, after all, had been the son of god also - the son of Osiris.

The minibus drew up and the door slid sideways to let us out. We were in a street where domed churches topped by crosses rose above the other buildings.

As time was limited Naguib had asked me which Coptic church I most wanted to see, and I'd told him the Church of St. Sergius. He now led the way down a deserted alleyway where only a middle-aged man wearing striped pyjamas stood, a solitary and immobile figure. The houses were narrow and, through an ancient open doorway, I glimpsed a young woman in an interior courtyard which was strung with lines of washing.

"Do you know," I said to Harry as we followed the others, "that the Christian Gnostics actually thought that the God of the Old Testament made false claims to power? According to a man called Valentinus who wrote the Gospel of Truth, there was a Higher Being who was the real divine source of all virtue, whilst God just gave commandments and judged and acted like a military dictator. I rather like the Gnostic idea."

"Never heard of Gnostic," said Harry. "Agnostic, but not Gnostic."

"Agnostic means 'not to know' and Gnostic means 'to know'. The fascinating thing is that these Gnostic

Christians were suppressed and declared heretics by the early Christian bishops. For all we know the whole movement of Christian thought as taught by those early bishops was a big mistake!"

"I doubt that very much," said Harry firmly.

We entered the Church of St. Sergius. It was built on the site where it was said the Holy Family had found refuge whilst in Egypt. The interior of this church was sober and quite unlike the Orthodox churches we'd visited in Greece with their glistening mosaics, frescoes and icons. This one had a low ceiling and stumpy ancient columns with Corinthian capitals supporting a gallery. Its main features were a sanctuary screen of geometric patterns of bone and ivory set in wood, and a marble pulpit with steps up to a long, raised dais whose sides were striped with inlays of different coloured marble, the dais itself being supported on many slim marble pillars.

Work was going on inside the church and a man was using an electric plane on a trapdoor set into the stone-flagged floor. Because he knew I was interested, Naguib had a word with the workman and I was invited to go down several steps to take a look at the crypt. It was there that it was believed the Holy Family had stayed three months. At the time there had been a Jewish community in the vicinity and it was natural that the Holy Family would have come to them. I used the strong arm of the workman to steady me as I picked my way over planks and general clobber, and descended half a dozen steep steps before metal pipes blocked my way. It was a good moment for the Almighty to give me a shove as divine punishment for thinking that he might be other than the supreme God. On the other hand, perhaps he found my questing the truth of him quite comical - especially as I was ready at a moment's notice to concede if I received a reprimand and was to fall head first into the crypt.

I didn't fall. There was no light down there so I could see little, but I managed to take a quite senseless photograph of props and paraphernalia. I say senseless because the print, when it was eventually developed, was a blotch and failed to reveal the ancient columns supporting stone archways shown in professional photographs which I'd seen in books.

Naguib smiled as I emerged. He was so willing to please that I now asked him if it was possible to see the Ben Ezra Synagogue which was nearby. "Of course," he replied. I hoped it also pleased the others but didn't ask.

The Ben Ezra had been built in the twelfth century over the site of a Christian church which itself had formerly been a synagogue. It was there that legend had it Pharaoh's daughter had found the baby Moses laid in the bulrushes.

Moses, like Jesus, had nearly been killed as an infant because the Pharaoh of the day had ordered the death of all male Hebrew children; he feared the increasing number of these Hebrew slaves, believing they would in time join with Egypt's enemies in war. Having been discovered in the bulrushes by Pharaoh's daughter, Moses was brought up in the palace and the Old Testament tells how he was later singled out by God to lead the Israelites from Egypt to their promised land.

God gave Moses commands and he performed extraordinary wizardry, outwitting all Pharaoh's magicians who tried their own brand of magic. God was proving his superior power over the Egyptian gods. Every time Moses demanded to be allowed to leave with his people, Pharaoh refused to let him go, whereupon God sent a plague that was so devastating that Pharaoh relented. But, according to the Book of Exodus, as soon as each plague was lifted, God deliberately hardened Pharaoh's heart so that he again refused to let the people go.

"It's only a story," Harry replied, when I commented that I thought it unreasonable of God to harden Pharaoh's heart. "Nothing worth worrying about."

"I can't understand why, if God wanted to get his 'chosen people' out, he didn't just take them out?" I remarked.

"God needed to show his power over Pharaoh's gods, I suppose," came the easy answer.

"So they did exist, those Egyptian gods?"

"Yes. No. Yes. No, of course not!"

"I mean, why did God turn the Nile water into blood, produce a plague of frogs and cause everyone to break out in boils, when all he had to do was soften Pharaoh's heart so his 'chosen people' could just slip away with Pharaoh's blessing? It would have caused much less misery."

"You're not going to change the Old Testament," said the wise one. "So you might as well just accept it."

The six pointed star of David stared down at us from the far wall of the synagogue. Nearby was a prominently placed marble stand engraved with gold lettering in Hebrew with a small skull-cap worn by Jews at prayer on either side, one white and one black.

Every synagogue has its holy ark, a cupboard where the Sefer Torah is kept (the Hebrew text of the Pentateuch in scroll form) the most hallowed possession of any synagogue. I supposed that it must be behind the brown doors which were inlaid with mother-of-pearl stars of various sizes.

The Jewish Passover originated in Egypt with the last plague. Moses received orders from God that each family was to kill a lamb and, before eating it, smear its blood on the door-posts and lintels. That way God would know to pass over the household because he intended to kill all the first-born of the Egyptian people. This event became the first Jewish Passover feast which, with the coming of Christianity, became the celebration of Easter.

In the atheistic lagoon of my mind I couldn't think how people could have faith in a God who sent plagues, and thought nothing of killing infants and annihilating those who didn't go along with his commands to worship him. That disasters overtook people and they put it down to sin and divine retribution seemed to me an eternal trap, a revolving wheel in which humans, like guinea-pigs, turned endlessly.

Naguib approached and asked pleasantly whether I wanted to see the El Amr Mosque, the first ever mosque in Egypt, built on the orders of the victorious General Amr ibn al-As in 641 A.D. "Wonderful! We're in your hands," I said, knowing at the same time that he and the others were somehow in mine, and hoping nobody cared too much.

"We go then," said Naguib.

The man in the striped pyjamas still stood in the alleyway. His face was expressionless and his arms hung at his sides like croquet mallets. I wouldn't want him to swing an arm at me, or at anyone else for that matter. We were all glad when we'd passed and were safely back in our minibus.

After a five minute drive, we drew up alongside the high crenellated exterior wall to the mosque, with its arched windows and finely sculptured entrance way. Naguib led the way through to the great courtyard with its canopied ablutions fountain. The mosque itself was undergoing structural repairs with a network of scaffolding amongst its two hundred columns supporting its multiple vaulted ceiling. One of the columns had been brought from Mecca and I asked Naguib which one it was. He waved an arm towards an inner area which was closed off for renovation. I would have liked to have seen it, if only because it was from the Holy City. A few Moslems were in the central area, one or two lying fully stretched out and asleep which seemed surprising, but maybe it wasn't the main prayer centre.

"Do you know why this mosque it is built here?" Naguib quizzed us as we wandered amongst the many columns. Seeing that none of us knew, he went on, "It is because General Amr, the victorious Moslem general in Egypt, when he comes with his army, he has his tent here and soon he finds in it a dove with her nest. He believes that it is Allah who has sent this dove, and it is here Allah wants a mosque so the people they can worship him."

A dove sitting on her eggs was, perhaps, significant because when Muhammed had had to flee Mecca, he had hidden in a mountain cave. His pursuers hadn't bothered to look inside the cave because an acacia tree had miraculously sprung up before its entrance with a dove peacefully sitting on her nest. As the mouth of the cave was above ground level and the dove had clearly not been disturbed, so his pursuers had passed on.

"Hope the dove was allowed to hatch her eggs," remarked the Brig, referring to the Cairo dove in General Amr's tent.

"Of course," said Naguib.

"Hum. Made a convenient pie for General Amr's dinner, no doubt," the Brig commented.

"Darling!" his wife rebuked him gently.

"Could do with some pigeon pie myself right now. We've been going all day with precious little to eat." Another accusing (but friendly) look was cast in my direction as if it was all my fault, which it clearly was. I had been toying with the thought of asking Naguib if we could drive on to the El Husayn Mosque, but realized that enough was enough for one day and I must abandon the idea. I didn't altogether give up hope, although I didn't know how it could be done as the following day we were setting off early for Alexandria, visiting desert monasteries on the way.

A tripod-mounted machine-gun manned by a soldier had its barrel pointing at us as we drove away from the check-point along the Alexandria desert road. We were amused by what to us was a mere game and diversion; we were innocent tourists in Egypt believing that, as we liked all the Egyptians we'd met so far, they were all our friends. We had no sense at all that as foreign travellers we might be shot.

We drove past banana plantations. Along the roadside were mimosa, palm trees and dusty firs. A slight haze hung like gauze in the sky. We again had Ali, who'd met us at the airport, as our guide. Now he pointed to a long low building and told us it was a prison. Between it and the road were acres of prickly pear.

"Wouldn't want to escape through that on a dark night. Very uncomfortable," commented the Brig.

"Oh, look, baby camels!" cried the Brig's wife. We all looked at the charming creatures as we drove past.

"And another dove-cote coming up - three of them!" she announced.

The dove-cotes were of baked mud and were like giant pepper-pots. We'd passed several of them but had seen no pigeons or doves.

"Now what?" demanded the Brig as a policeman flagged us down. Here they had a Yellow Maria parked by the roadside.

Our driver got out and after a lengthy discussion returned looking sheepish. He had a few words with Ali who told us that the police had given him a warning about speeding and driving in the middle of the road instead of on the right. We drove on, the driver obeying the orders until out of sight of the police, when he reverted to speeding and taking to the middle of the road again.

After an hour's drive we turned left heading for the Wadi Natrun desert monasteries. We passed through a village with the desert stretching in all directions. A tall minaret reminded everyone of prayer.

A few miles further and we were stopped by security police at the entrance to the Monastery of Anba Bishoi hidden within an oasis of palms and greenery. There were more questions and answers before we were waved on to park beside the high sand-coloured walls of the monastery. Ali led the way in and, whilst we waited for him to get tickets, two bearded monks in their black robes approached down a long corridor. One of them had a close fitting black bonnet decorated with small white crosses, the other was elderly with a white beard, black hood and a wooden staff. I wondered if he was the Abbot.

We were led through narrow passages and up steps and across a drawbridge till we came out onto a flat roof. From there we could look around at the many buildings, to domes, bell-towers and to the massive el-Suriani Monastery. Beyond the green trees and cultivation lay the desert stretching to the horizon.

Monasticism was first started by Christians in the deserts of Egypt in the third century. St. Antony (c.251-356 A.D.) had been one of the first. I'd very much wanted to visit his monastery near the Red Sea, but it had been an impracticable idea. I could have pursued the plan relentlessly had there been more time, more freedom, more money and less spouse control. As things stood I had to be content with St. Bishoi.

Wadi Natrun gets its name from the deposits of natron found there which was used in ancient times for mummifying corpses. Thirty-six miles further north St. Antony first founded a colony of hermits at a place called Cellia where there are numerous saline lakes around which the natron deposits are to be found.

According to Coptic tradition the Holy Family passed through Wadi Natrun and Jesus foretold 'spiritual fighters' living there. His passing through was said to fulfil Isaiah's words: 'Behold, the Lord is riding on a swift cloud and comes to Egypt; and the idols of Egypt will tremble at his presence, and the heart of the Egyptians will melt within them.' (Isaiah 19:1). The general idea being that the Virgin Mary was the cloud on which Jesus came because she was like the whitest cloud, and as pure and light and lofty as one.

I said to Harry that it could as easily be interpreted to refer to – well, me, as we'd flown out of the clouds; or to Alexander the Great who'd come to Egypt and had been revered as a god and to whom the idols of Egypt had every cause to tremble. But Harry told me not to mess about with what was the accepted interpretation.

The pattern for asceticism had been set by St. Makarius of Alexandria when, in about 373 A.D., he had settled in a solitary cell beside the nearby natron lakes. Numerous anchorites followed him, all living apart but meeting on Sundays for prayer. Their fasting and abstinence were greatly admired. It is said that Makarius was once extremely distressed at having killed a gnat and, as a penance, he took himself off to some marshes 'where there were flies whose powerful stings were sufficient to pierce the hide of a wild boar'. There he remained six months 'till his body was so much disfigured that his brethren on his return only knew him by the sound of his voice'. He was a notorious faster and only on Sundays did he indulge in a raw cabbage-leaf which earned him many admirers.

A monk in black habit and bonnet with the twelve small white crosses on it (representing the twelve disciples) joined us for a short while on the roof. He told us that the earliest monks had had such love of God that they'd been driven from the cities to get away from the pagan gods of Egypt. St. Bishoi (whose monastery we were in) had come about 340 A.D. His mother had known he was destined to serve God because an angel had told her before he was even born.

I felt sure I should have many questions to ask him, but for once I couldn't think of any. Anyway, the monk continued without pause - he was clearly used to briefing visitors. There were currently, he said, a hundred and fifty-eight monks in all and twenty novices. That sounded an impressive number. They began the day at three every morning with prayers in their cells, before joining in communal worship at four a.m. The rest of the day they attended to their various duties which included manual labour. Communal worship began again in the early evening. The monks of this monastery were coenobitic, which meant they lived together and shared their possessions. I would have liked to have asked what they prayed about during all those hours but thought it would be impolite.

He took us to the other side of the roof where we looked out over several sand-coloured domes topped by crosses. He pointed to them and informed us that whenever the Coptic Patriarch visited Wadi Natrun that was where he stayed. A newly elected Patriarch, who is sometimes called Pope in the Coptic Church, was always selected from the monks of St. Antony's Monastery near the Red Sea. Far from being illiterate, as many people might expect, many who joined the monastery today were from professional backgrounds and had computer skills.

The Brig was far more interested in a large mill-wheel he'd spotted down below, and wanted to know where it had come from. The monk was prepared to enquire for him and led us down to ground level again. I left them investigating the mill-wheel and went off to explore the monastery alone.

I looked in at the main Church of St. Bishoi where I found a crowd of excited and chattering school children. It was there that St. Bishoi's embalmed body lay under a red shroud. A wooden canopy, inlaid with intricate patterns of ivory crosses, was raised over him. I would have liked to have taken a closer look but the school children were summoned to stand before his catafalque for a photo opportunity. It is said that being so holy his body had remained uncorrupted and, whenever a truly devout person stood beside him, he sometimes stretched an arm out from his shroud to shake the person's hand. I wondered what he might do to someone playing the atheist and was quite pleased that the school children remained between him and me.

I left the church and went down a long barrel-roofed passageway, at the bottom of which I came to a courtyard which was obviously the monastery cemetery. Along one side wall were many square recesses marked with plaques giving in Arabic the names, dates of death and portraits of the deceased monks. Some recesses were empty, ready to receive, I supposed, future bones or bodies.

According to a book about the Coptic Church in Egypt, the cult of the dead today is as important as it was in ancient Egypt. A ceremony called Rakh'ma is held three times a year, when the relatives gather at the monastery and distribute bread and the favourite food of the deceased to the poor in the deceased's name. They pay the priest to pray for the soul of their relative and to burn incense before his tomb.

Two monks were standing before one of the memorial plaques. I must have smiled at them because they greeted me, though only one spoke English. Yes, this was the cemetery, he said, and pointed to one of the portraits. It was of his uncle, he told me. He had come all the way from Aswan and his companion was his brother. I felt I was intruding and, like the chameleon which I always was in the presence of the devout, I put on my holy colours and felt as holy as I'd ever felt anywhere.

"It is God's love that binds us all," the monk said.

"Yes, of course," I replied, fawning under my cloak of a true believer. "God's love binds us all." And I bowed my way backwards until I was out of sight. Once I was gone, my holy colours quickly faded as everyday concerns, such as where were the others, and pangs of hunger, took over.

"So where is St. Antony's Monastery?" asked the Brig, with a look defying me to get our driver to take us to it.

"About six hours drive going in the opposite direction," I answered. We were back in the minibus.

"Not to have your family around you!" remarked his wife. She wasn't referring to St. Antony's Monastery but Wadi Natrun where we'd just been.

"One way of getting away from them," declared the Brig.

"To think of spending your whole life there!"

"It's the ascetics who I find so odd," I said. "Living alone in the desert and starving themselves to a state of madness."

"Couldn't help themselves once they'd got the bug," said the Brig. "Once one did it then it was as infectious as measles."

As we sped on along the desert road I thought about St. Antony and the extraordinary life he'd led. Athanasius, bishop of Alexandria in 328 A.D., had encouraged the ascetic movement in Egypt and had written a 'Life of Antony'. In it he'd described how people coming across the desert to St. Antony's Monastery could sometimes hear 'a tumultuous rout within, bawling and wailing...' which was St. Antony wrestling with the devil. The devil renewed his assaults night and day and 'threw filthy thoughts into his mind', but St. Antony 'routed them out as fast by prayer'.

Perhaps the passage I liked the best in Athanasius' 'Life' was when two philosophers came to see him in his cell to test him. Antony merely asked them why they were bothering to come to see him as he was such 'a simple fellow'. He said: "'If you come to a silly fellow, your labour is lost, and to no purpose. But if ye think otherwise, become such as I am, for we should imitate all things that are fair and commendable. Had I come to you, I would have imitated you. Since therefore you come to me, become such men as I am, for I am a Christian.'" But they, whilst admiring Antony, 'withdrew, for they saw the devils dreading Antony.'

St. Antony had made a point of seeing the good in everyone and absorbing it to himself. In another interview between him and some men who had come to 'scoff at him, because he hadn't learnt to read', he'd asked them which they thought the most important, the mind or the alphabet? They'd replied the mind, of course, because it had been the inventor of letters, to which Antony had said: ' "Who has a sound mind, stands in no need of letters" ', and the men had gone away full of admiration because Antony had been so 'courteous and civil and not savage like a mountaineer despite his years in the desert.'

In his biography Athanasius wrote also how St. Antony had hoped for martyrdom and had deliberately attended a court in Alexandria to give encouragement to Christians who were standing trial there. The Judge ordered him to leave but St. Antony, hoping for martyrdom, didn't obey and instead 'stood foremost on an high place before the Judge's face.' Much to his disappointment the glory of martyrdom was denied him and he'd had to leave Alexandria and return to the desert where he lived until he was over a hundred years old.

Well, we were on our way to Alexandria now. I was looking forward to seeing the city which had once been a centre for religious debates and philosophical discussions.

"Today's catch, Ali?" enquired the Brig.

"Of course," he replied with a smile of happiness that he had sprung this unexpected and memorable meal on us. As we'd approached Alexandria from El Alamein, passing reed-fringed lakes where the odd punt was being poled by turban headed figures, and where in the distance tall oil refinery chimneys belched flames, Ali had suddenly enquired whether we'd like to visit a small fish restaurant he knew of in the back streets of Alexandria. The Brig and his wife jumped at the idea and Harry and I were honour bound to fall in with the plan.

Secretly I would have preferred a good grilled steak but, having dragged the Brig and his wife around the Coptic quarter of Cairo, the least I could do was to fall in line with them now.

The minibus took us down the narrow back streets of Alexandria and parked up on the pavement outside a grotty looking café. The thickset, black moustached Egyptian proprietor, in jeans and open neck shirt revealing his black hairy chest had, I think, been forewarned of our arrival on a mobile as he appeared to be waiting outside for us.

A large ice-chest on wheels stood in the street and the lid was raised for our inspection. It contained rows of fish of all sizes with their glazed eyes staring at us. Bluebottles buzzed around our heads as we were invited to select the fish we fancied. I chose one that looked plump and was told it was snapper.

We entered the restaurant which looked like a public convenience with white tiled walls, and sat down at two square tables covered by white oilcloths. A few house flies flew around aimlessly waiting for something to settle on. Bead curtains hung before two recessed hand basins. Several dubious looking characters sat at other tables. Hygiene and germs were always foremost in our thoughts whenever we ate abroad, but there was no escape.

When our food came the skin of my fish was well charred and the staring eye didn't bother me. I noticed Harry with a sick expression as he cut off the head of his fish and hid it under a sliced tomato.

"This is where we all go down with gippy tummy," growled the Brig, voicing our anxieties.

The Brig's wife was expert at filleting out the backbone of whatever it was she had. The Brig had a plateful of shrimps, prawns and squid. I thought he was really asking for trouble but, according to his wife, he never got stomach problems and could eat anything. We were the whimps, both of us equally suspicious. Harry played about with morsels of food and I saw him gulp as his fish eye suddenly stared up at him when the sliced tomato shifted. Concealing it under two slices of tomato he courageously ate a few onion rings and some rice. I was more afraid of betraying my whimpishness and so ate all mine, comforted by the knowledge that we had pills to counter any ill effects.

The conversation centred around the British War Cemetery at El-Alamein where we'd been that afternoon. The site was about thirty miles from Alexandria. Its rows of headstones filled a wide depression in the desert and stretched into the distance in all directions. There had been something poignant, desolate and poetic in its isolation. I'd examined some inscriptions and had paused before those unnamed 'known unto God' only.

Leaving the others talking about desert warfare and campaign tactics, I'd walked down a path between the rows of headstones to a chapel where a giant cross was raised high against the skyline. Carefully tended shrubs of Bougainvillaea bloomed either side of the gravelled pathway.

The chapel had been locked and I'd peered through the window but could see little. Whilst alive the 'Known Unto God' would have had a name and rank; his existence would have been important to his family and would have made some sort of impact on anyone who'd known him. Undoubtedly at some stage, when shot and dying, his prayers or cries or screams would have included the word 'God'.

Nobody ever screams out 'Holy Spirit!', only 'God!' or 'Christ!' It was odd how we were all grounded in the word 'God', and yet it was the spirit that was an endless source of energy and could be tapped from the depth of being like a pure spring.

"A plate for our fish-bones!" cried the Brig.

"I get for you," said Ali.

A clean plate was brought and the fish heads and bones were off-loaded onto it. The plate was centrally placed and numerous eyes now stared accusingly at Harry who stopped eating altogether.

"Don't you like your fish?" the Brig's wife asked Harry. "Look, there's heaps of rice, have some more of it."

"Probably doesn't like the eyes!" said the Brig, assessing the matter accurately.

Harry mumbled something about 'fresh fish, nothing like it!'

"Wonder what fish see with their eyes. D'you think they see knives and forks picking into them?"

"Don't, darling. It doesn't bear thinking of."

"Do you have National Service in Egypt?" I asked Ali,

to draw attention away from Harry's plight.

"Yes, we have."

"Done yours, have you?" asked the Brig.

"Yes. For one year I do mine."

"Any action?"

"No. All I remember is I have to carry a bazooka."

"Huh! A bazooka! Wouldn't want to be behind anybody firing that!" the Brig said. "Fire and brimstone, hm? Wouldn't want to be in front of it either," he added

Whilst at El-Alamein I'd asked Ali if his father had fought in the war. I didn't think about the age gap between us. He'd replied that he'd fought in the 1973 war.

The 1973 war? I'd racked my brains trying to remember what war that was. At the El-Alamein museum I'd been surprised, when trying to find a book on the desert campaigns, to find only postcards celebrating the glorious 1973 Egyptian victory against Israel. I couldn't remember any victory and was only dimly aware of Arab defeats. I've since learned it was the Yom Kippur War. Then, in conjunction with Syria, the Egyptians had launched a campaign against Israel to which Israel had immediately responded with all her military might. The only victory for Egypt had been that she'd regained the Sinai peninsula which had been lost to the Israelis in the 1967 Six Day War.

The Brig put his napkin down on the table. "Has everybody finished, then?" He regarded Harry's mound of food still concealing his fish head, tail and most of the body. Harry made a vague gesture of being replete and managed the ghost of a smile, encouraged by the knowledge that we were at last going on to a many starred, decidedly classy hotel which must have some standard of hygiene attached to it.

"Then let's get going. Cecil Hotel, here we come!" cried the Brig.

We paid the bill and bowed to the proprietor's hairy chest with words of praise regarding his small establishment. Soon we were on our way, smoothing out the many creases in our clothes to make ourselves look more respectable after a day's travelling. We ignored the police with sub-machine guns outside the Cecil and went bleeping through the metal detector placed inside the hotel entrance.

The Cecil Hotel was famous for having had such varied guests as Churchill and Noel Coward, Lawrence Durrell and Somerset Maugham. Cleopatra, so it is claimed, killed herself on its doorstep, though how that came about I'm not quite sure as it wasn't built until 1930. It had spacious, lofty rooms, many columns, plaster mouldings and antiquated wrought iron lifts with gleaming brass fitments. My major concern was to remain dignified whilst clinging to my blue sun-hat full of uneaten rolls from our picnic lunch; I had to make a mental note not to put it absent-mindedly on my head.

But I wasn't in Alexandria for the hotel, I was there for its history. It had once been a melting-pot of Greek philosophical thought, early Christianity, paganism, and Judaism before the Moslems swept in in the seventh century. It is said that Christianity was brought to Egypt by St. Mark who is believed to have come to the Jewish community in Alexandria about 43 A.D. Had I been free to explore Alexandria on my own I'd have searched out the site where there'd once been an early church, the Church of St. Mark, near to the Eastern Harbour. St. Mark is regarded by the Copts as the first Patriarch of the Coptic Church. His successors lived originally in Alexandria, though the seat of the Coptic Patriarch today is in Cairo, and St. Mark's relics are now also in Cairo in the Cathedral of St. Mark.

"Pity we never saw the relics of St. Mark," I said to Harry, when we had bowed to our liveried page, who'd just brought up our luggage, and had given him a tip befitting the Cecil Hotel and its illustrious past.

"Relics?" asked Harry, "who wants to see relics?

"I do."

"I don't want to see a lot of bones."

"St. Mark's bones? I'd have liked to have seen the Patriarch in Cairo too."

"Why on earth would you want to see the Patriarch in Cairo? You saw a Patriarch in Istanbul." He made them sound like a rare species of animal, which in a way they were.

I was too tired to argue the matter. All I knew at that precise moment was that, despite all the historical wonders of ancient Alexandria, I didn't want to see anything. After all the driving that day I felt I was still travelling; the furniture kept moving strangely, as though it was passing, and the bedroom floor was undulating gently. I would have liked to have taken a caleche and gone trotting along the Corniche to get a sniff of Alexandria's night life. But there was only one place I was going to and that was straight to bed.

By next morning we felt rejuvenated. We were celebrating the fact that we were still well after the fish restaurant the previous night. We could face the day with confidence. After breakfast we were put in the care of Fatima, a charming young woman with the Moslem head covering and wearing a long light-weight coat. She immediately informed us that she had a bad cold and hoped she wouldn't lose her voice.

The Brig remarked: "Didn't know Egyptians caught colds." His wife was consoling. "We know just how beastly colds can be. You should take honey for it."

I tried to say something kind but felt more concerned about not getting it myself.

We were driven to the museum. On the way Fatima popped a lozenge in her mouth before giving us an outline of Alexander the Great's policy on his arrival in Egypt in 332 B.C. With Persian occupation at that time the Egyptians looked on him as a saviour not a conqueror because he'd driven the Persians out. She told us how Alexander had taken the title of Pharaoh and had sacrificed to the local gods at Memphis, the ancient capital of Egypt. He'd wanted Egyptian co-operation and, with this in mind, he'd brilliantly combined Egyptian and Greek gods so that people worshipped together in unity and peace. One of the most important gods at the time had been Amun whom Alexander identified with Zeus.

Fatima cleared her throat and turned her head away from us to cough and blow her nose. Croakily she continued: "Have you heard of the Siwa Oasis?" I was about to say I had but she quickly shut her eyes, raised her head and fumbled for and found a handkerchief before she was convulsed by a sneeze.

"Ahhhh! Excuse me," she said. "I'm about to explain to you that Siwa it is six hours drive from Alexandria. It is a long way. There is there the ancient oracle of the god Amun whom Alexander worshipped as the Greek god Zeus. When Alexander he comes to Egypt, he travels five hundred miles to the Siwa Oasis to consult the oracle of

Amun." She rearranged her flowing head-dress to make sure no strand of hair was showing. "When Alexander he arrives at Siwa he goes to the temple of Amun where he is greeted by the high priest as 'the son of God'. Now this is not so surprising because Alexander has given himself the title of Pharaoh and, as you know, the Pharaoh was believed by the people to be Horus, the son of Osiris. But already Alexander he is seeing himself as the son of Zeus, supreme god of all the Greek gods." She stopped to give another sharp explosive sneeze. I'd read somewhere that the germs from a sneeze could scatter a hundred yards. I obviously hadn't a hope of avoiding her cold.

"Excuse me!" She blew her nose before continuing. "The Macedonian kings believe themselves to be descended from Zeus, but to be descended is not the same as being the son of the god. And do you know how old Alexander is when he arrives in Egypt? He is twenty years old. Only twenty years of age! Can you imagine that? Can you imagine a young man of twenty commanding his generals, his armies, and conquering all these lands when he is only twenty years old? He has to be a god, do you not think?" She regarded us all with her beautiful rheumy eyes, her nostrils twitching. "So now we are here at the museum. We will see only a part of it, but if you will keep close to me so I do not have to speak loud or I lose my voice. I want to show you what I think are the most interesting things for you."

She led the way - to what, I have forgotten, except for two things which stamped themselves on my memory. One was a mummified body with a cross painted at the neck, symbolic of the new Christian religion. The ancient Egyptian hieroglyph of the ankh was very similar to the Christian cross but with a loop at the top; it represented eternal life and had always been easily recognized by the illiterate. It was an obvious symbol for Christians and was adopted by the Egyptian Coptic Church.

The other impressive exhibit was the Apis bull, a giant statue of a vigorous animal with the sun disc of the god Ra between its horns. It had been brought from the temple of Serapis where it had been erected in the second century A.D. to commemorate the Emperor Hadrian's visit to Alexandria. Serapis was a fusion of Osiris and the Apis bull combined with a number of Greek gods, but in particular Dionysos whose symbol had been a bull representing power and fertility.

The cult of the Apis bull was decidedly odd. He was the ba (personality) of the god Ptah, the creator god of Memphis, who was usually portrayed as a mummy with his hands protruding (like St. Bishoi from his shroud), holding a sort of sceptre which included the ankh sign. There could always be only one Apis bull at a time. It was carefully selected for its markings and revered because its life was closely associated with the Pharaoh. The mother cow of the Apis bull (as with the mother of the Pharaoh) was also venerated as she was believed to be a manifestation of the goddess Isis, and on its death the Apis, like the Pharaoh, was identified with the god Osiris. After their years in Egypt the Israelites would have known the cult of the Apis and there is a theory that, when Moses came down with the tablets of the ten commandments and found his Israelites worshipping a golden calf, it might well have been them reverting to the Apis bull, hoping to gain relief from their sufferings in the wilderness.

The museum had a shady garden and café where Fatima gave us half an hour to recover our wits after our two hour tour. I gave up on avoiding her cold and sat with her on a stone seat under a tree. I asked her if she'd mind if I put some questions to her about Islam and to whisper her answers.

Had she done the hajj, the pilgrimage to Mecca which was required at least once in the lifetime of each Moslem? No, she had not, she whispered, because the cost was about four thousand pounds sterling. But one day she hoped to have saved enough to make the journey.

"How can poor people afford it?" I asked.

She turned quickly away and blew her nose before explaining in a croaky whisper that those who couldn't afford it could apply to the government. They had to apply every year and priority was given to the older applicants. As for those who were not poor, they must keep saving towards it.

As we were alone I asked her about the problems they had faced in Egypt regarding tourism after 9/11. That was terrible for everyone in Egypt who depended on the tourist trade, she told me. She had had no work for several months and if it hadn't been for her husband, who was in the oil industry, her family would have gone bankrupt. "Now things are better," she whispered. "We hope not to have any more problems like that."

I asked her one more question. I told her I was fascinated by Christian saints who, I'd read or heard, were often petitioned by Moslems regarding health or fertility. Was this true, I asked?

"Yes, but that is a wrong thing in Islam," she replied. She sounded like an adolescent boy whose voice was breaking. "For a Moslem to pray to a Christian saint and to rub her hands over the tombstone to ask for a miracle is not right. Only Allah can bring about a miracle and a

Moslem should always pray only to Allah. Allah is always there for each person, there is no need for the saint to intercede. If you are very ill there is no requirement for you to prostrate yourself, Allah knows you are too ill and so you pray with your eyes and your mind without action. You must understand Islam is a very simple religion. You must believe and submit only to Allah."

I liked what she told me - to submit! It was very simple and just meant letting go. And that meant letting go of everything, including questions, doubts and possibilities.

We were driven to the ancient Serapeum where we were taken through a shady area of trees and then put in the care of a strange individual. For some reason this middle-aged man immediately abducted me and, taking my arm in a vice-like grip, he marched me briskly over the uneven ground to Pompey's pillar flanked by its four sphinxes. The column had, in fact, been dedicated to the Emperor Diocletian in around 300 A.D. but had been wrongly called Pompey's pillar by medieval travellers. It is believed that it might once have been part of the original portico to the great temple of Serapis which crowned the small hill.

Gripping my arm, the man with great gusto marched me around Pompey's pillar, did a figure of eight around the sphinxes and, without pause, marched me on to the remains of the Serapeum. Soon we had disappeared down into an underground passageway. He pointed to various things and kept repeating the words 'very good' between grunts of satisfaction. I thought that, as I was captive it was an opportunity to try out a bit of Arabic. But 'very good' was the only answer I got as he huffed and puffed and sweated profusely, marching me to the end of one underground passageway, then to the end of another where he then bowed repeatedly to a bit of rock and made me do the same.

Where were the others? What had been quite amusing was becoming insane. The man had no sense of caution and seemed to be fired with an unstoppable zest and energy. Having done repeated bows to the rock with explanations which I couldn't understand, he turned me about and marched me back triumphantly, pointing to several niches in the rock and repeatedly rasping out the Arabic word 'kitab' which I knew meant 'book'. It had, apparently, or so I learned later, been part of the Great Alexandrian Library. As he marched me out again I was glad to see Harry and the others approaching.

"Ah, there you are! We were beginning to get worried," said the Brig's wife placidly.

"You should have waited for - ," Harry began, but I was already gone again, my abductor renewing the grip on my arm and marching me back down the hill along the uneven ground to Fatima who was resting under a tree.

After my release, I asked Fatima why I'd been made to bow at the end of the tunnel, and she told me that it was the ancient altar to Serapis.

The Serapeum had been rebuilt and greatly enlarged by the Emperor Hadrian (117-138 A.D.), suggesting that Christianity had hitherto made little impact. By 250 A.D., however, the Christians were becoming an organized institution and a force to be reckoned with. The Roman emperors were getting irritated by Christian insistence that they alone held the right beliefs. Persecutions came to a climax under the Emperor Diocletian (284-305 A.D.) Unlike Alexander the Great's policy of unifying with Egyptian gods, Christians insisted that their religion was the only valid truth and there could be no compromise. Tertullian, a second century Church Father from Carthage, said that because - because! - Christianity was so unbelievable, it had to be believed!

Then, hey presto! Constantine the Great suddenly accepted Christianity. He had paganism and Christianity running side by side. He was considerate regarding his pagan subjects but, by the end of the century under the Emperor Theodosius I, there was no such toleration. Theodosius forbade sacrifice and pagan worship was outlawed. Now it was the Christian turn to persecute. In 391 A.D. a large Christian mob came to the Serapeum led by Theophilus, the Patriarch, and totally destroyed the temple. The death of St. Mark who, according to the Coptic Church, had been lynched in Alexandria by the worshippers of Serapis, was well and truly avenged. Perhaps it had happened where we were sitting quietly now?

"Isn't it odd," I said to Fatima, "how people persecute and murder in the name of religion?"

"Yes, it is not good," came the croaky response.

Soon we were driving along the Corniche with its elegant houses and palm trees on one side and the Mediterranean on the other. After a while we came to a long, low building with a sloping expanse of glass which was divided up to give a honeycomb effect. This building and others nearby, Fatima informed us, were part of the new library built on the site of the ancient Alexandrian Library founded by the first Ptolemy.

She asked the driver to stop and, holding her

handkerchief near to her nose, Fatima told us how the Ptolemies, keen to promote their Hellenistic culture, had built the old Library and Museum which had become the greatest centre of learning in the ancient world.

"Ph - ph - ph - ." Each time she began the word she couldn't complete it. "Excuse me!" Handkerchief to nose - big blow - another clean handkerchief recovered from her handbag. "I want to tell you that philosophy, mathematics and the sciences, they all flourish here and scholars from all over the known world they come to Alexandria to increase their knowledge. The translation of the Old Testament into Greek - the Septuagint you say because it was done by seventy-two Jewish scholars sent here to Alexandria to do the translation - it was done at the order of Ptolemy II, so they can have here in their great library the law of the Jews. At that time Greek is the language of the educated classes. As you know also the New Testament is first written in Greek."

"Wasn't there a school in Alexandria that taught Christianity?" I asked, remembering in the dim recesses of my mind that I'd read something about one.

"You are thinking of Clement of Alexandria, one of the earliest Christians who lives here. Yes, he is head of the Catechetical School in 190 A.D. It is interesting you read him because he writes against the Greek gods who, he says, are not gods but poetic fancy."

I'd read some of Clement's harangues against the Hellenic deities. He thought the Egyptian gods far better as many of them were only animals, whilst the Greek ones he accused of being 'adulterous and lewd'.

I thought it a shame as I quite enjoyed the wild and joyful abandonment of the Greek gods. The Christian emphasis on sin seemed claustrophobic in comparison. Not that I particularly wanted to sin, but Christian theologians always assumed one had succumbed in one way or another and needed to be redeemed. In fact, I often thought that bishops and priests depended on the sin of their flocks so that they could draw them conscience-stricken into the fold and hold them captive to their need for forgiveness.

"So what about Cleopatra? Was she smooching with Antony behind papyrus scrolls in the library?" asked the Brig.

Fatima said, "I tell you one minute, please. First, about the library, you should know that Alexandria it is so important a city at the time of the Ptolemies, that everybody in the world comes. And do you know that at the time there is a law that, if there is a ship coming to Alexandria and on it there is a papyrus scroll, the ship it cannot leave until the scroll has been copied for the library? By the first century B.C. the library has more than half a million manuscripts! Now you ask about Cleopa-pa-pa-pa- " Fatima enveloped her nose in a handkerchief. "Ah! Excuse me!"

"Definitely a whisky!" growled the Brig.

"Honey and lemon," said his wife.

"To tell you about Cleopatra," said Fatima, "you know they have found her palace in the Eastern Harbour? It is underwater where it has been since several earthquakes from the fourth century. It is found in 1996 by a French marine archaeologist. Can you imagine the earthquakes that caused this? Such terrible earthquakes so that the whole palace is lost in the sea? To answer your question whether Cleopatra is smooching - what is this word smooch?"

"Embracing," said the Brig.

"Smooch. I like the word and will remember that I first learn it when looking at our new library. Do you have your photographs you want?" she asked. "No? We are not allowed to park here, but a few minutes will not matter."

I took advantage of the few minutes, feeling that this had been the nerve-centre of Alexandria, where the flux of opinions had come together and sifted out through heated debate. At the time that Christianity was seeping slowly into the pagan mind there had flourished in Alexandria the Neoplatonist school of philosophy under Plotinus. His student, Porphyry, was believed to have once become a Christian but had then become more convinced by the Neoplatonist idea of a hierarchy of existence. His belief was that there at the summit was the One or the Good, and beneath it the world of Ideas, and below that the World Soul. It was this World Soul that created the material things and which ordered the universe. Individuals got their soul from the World Soul and, by contemplation, could find union with God (The One or The Good).

Apart from finding the works of Plotinus totally incomprehensible, the idea of a World Soul seemed to me a good idea. Porphyry had admired Christ but he regarded his failure to be saved on the cross as proof that he wasn't divine.

It was here at Alexandria, of course, that the divinity of Jesus became a major topic of controversy. Athanasius, bishop of Alexandria 328 A.D. was irate with Arius, the priest of the Church of St. Mark, because he was asserting that Jesus as the Son of God was less than God, as opposed to Athanasius' insistence that he was of the same substance as God, both divine and human. Added to this was now the Coptic belief that Jesus was wholly divine and not human at all which led finally to the Copts breaking with the main body of the Church in 451 A.D. The nature of Christ was banged on about for a number of centuries, almost as though Christ himself didn't matter, but the winning of arguments did.

Under the Byzantine Empire there was gradually a systematic destruction of temples due entirely to Christian intolerance of paganism. Some think the burning of the great Alexandrian Library and Museum was done by the Christians whose only intention was to reduce paganism to dust and ashes. St. Cyril, the Patriarch at the start of the fifth century, had a hatred for Jews and persecuted them, before finally expelling them from the city. So everybody, far from following Christ's teaching that they should love one another - or at least forgive one another - seemed rather more to hate each other without reservation.

St. Cyril also got himself embroiled in the dispute over the word Theotokos for the Virgin Mary. Was she a god-bearer as the title implied, or a man-bearer? The pagan goddess Isis had been mother of a god and it was dangerous for Christianity to make the Virgin Mary similar. It's interesting that Christianity in Egypt was a sort of replica of the old Egyptian pagan idea of a son of god, a resurrection and divine judgement.

"Everybody's waiting for you," said Harry, taking the camera from me. I'd strayed further than I'd meant and we hurried back to the minibus where we found the Brig instructing Fatima in the use of the word 'smooch'. No, she jolly well couldn't smooch Muhammed or the Imam at the mosque. Smooch is more a hands-on sort of love and has to be used in the right context.

"But you say Cleopatra smooches with papyrus scrolls and Antony?" she asked, mystified.

"Smooched with Antony amongst papyrus scrolls. You must get - What must she get, old girl?" he asked his wife.

"Don't ask me, darling! Get it right, that's all."

We joined the traffic again, passing occasional caleches bowling along. The horses all appeared well groomed, contented and well fed, with their cheerful colourful trappings; the passengers, peering out from the black cabs, also had an air of being contented and well fed. Fatima spoke about the arrival of the Moslems and their effect on the Alexandrians. She smiled sweetly as she told us that the Koran forbade intolerance of other religions and ordered that Moslems treat the vanquished with kindness. I'd read a sentence in the Koran which said: 'There shall be no compulsion in religion'. Well, no compulsion there might have been, but a poll-tax had, nevertheless, been levied on all Copts and they were forbidden to ride a horse (presumably so they couldn't look down on Moslems).

"And by the year eight or nine hundred A.D.," went on Fatima, "the total population who become Moslem are eighty percent."

"What happened to the Copts during the Crusades?" asked the Brig.

"Ah, that is difficult for the Coptic people. Because of their Christian beliefs they like to support the Crusaders on the one hand but, because they are Egyptian, they want also to support the Moslems. You must remember that they are broken away from the mother Church. But remember also that the Copts are not unhappy with the coming of the Moslems to Egypt. This is because the Moslems free them from the repressive Byzantine Empire. The Orthodox Christian emperors of Byzantium do not tolerate the Coptic Church because it has broken from them. One minute, please!" She blew her nose discreetly, bending her head almost down to her lap. "As you know, the Orthodox

Church it also breaks away from the Catholic Church. And so on and so forth - so on and so forth - is this what you say in England? So on, so forth?"

"Absolutely spot on," said the Brig.

"Spot on? Spo-o-o-o-o- " She convulsed down into her lap where she stayed for several minutes.

"Poor woman should be in bed," said the Brig's wife sympathetically.

"Knows how to get it out of her system all right," the Brig muttered.

When the head came up she caught sight of our final destination. "Ah, this is the Montazah Palace!" she said. "As you can see it is not old but it is the crazy fantasy of..." And we did a circuit around the final reaches of the Corniche where the wealth of an ancestor of King Farouk had allowed him to carve out for himself his own man-made bay for his own solitary swim, and his own private marina and whatever else had been his fancy.

"Three forty-five wake up call? Hum!" commented the Brig as he helped himself to some vegetables.

"They say it's because planes are flying in from Saudi with Moslems coming back from Mecca," said his wife. "I suppose they have to be given priority."

"Don't see why," said the Brig.

"You don't think there's another reason altogether and they're trying not to alarm us?" I suggested. "Did you hear the air-raid siren this afternoon? And didn't you say there's trouble brewing in Baghdad?"

I was given a sharp look. "You think we're going to be flown back home?" questioned the Brig.

"Could be."

"End of the hols? Pity. I've been looking forward to relaxing on the Nile for a few days."

Harry said something about having to have his early morning tea before going anywhere. I had completely hashed up our tea making equipment which was Harry's lifeline to sanity whilst abroad. Instead of putting the element into the water, I'd hung it outside the metal pot and it had blown. After the intense activity of the past few days I was clearly no longer in full command of my senses.

"Surely the Cecil Hotel will wake us up with tea?" I said. I wasn't sure whether the hotel mightn't be above doing such things. Cocktails, champagne and oysters served to the upper echelons of society were much more their scene. "Make sure they do!" commented the Brig. "Won't go anywhere without my early morning tea."

"Darling, you never drink tea in the morning."

"I will tomorrow. If Harry does, I don't see why I can't?"

"I agree it sounds nice," said his wife.

"Tea it is, then," the Brig announced.

I was also looking forward to the three nights cruising on the Nile and comparative inertia. But, if there was a sudden change of plan, an Islamic terrorist uprising, an expected storming of all minibuses carrying foreign tourists, well, so be it. Ali's anxious expression when he'd informed us that we were having to get up in the early hours, never betrayed for a moment that there was any political problem underlying this change of plan. But then it wasn't in his interest to give away the true facts. I think he was relieved that we all took it calmly and didn't rant and rave and demand to see his manager.

By this time the next day then, we would either find

ourselves back at Heathrow or cruising on the Nile. Only time would tell.

The sun was up but there was a faint mist hanging over Cairo as we drove through the suburbs to the Citadel. The Citadel was an impressive legacy whose original construction had been begun by Saladin, the renowned Moslem whose army recaptured Jerusalem from the Christians at the time of the Crusades in the twelfth century.   From behind the Citadel's thick stone walls, several mosques with their minarets rose supreme to show the triumph of the Moslem faith.

We drew up and got out into the cool early morning air. The Brig stumped around and did a military reconnoitre, whilst his wife took photographs of the occasional donkey and cart on the otherwise deserted road.

Ali came up to me and said: "I have not forgotten you want to see the El-Husayn Mosque, we will see that also."

I could have kissed him. It was well worth getting up at three forty-five if, after the Citadel, we were to be taken to the mosque.

The El-Husayn Mosque was far from being the oldest, but was of great importance in the Moslem world. It was where the Moslem faithful flocked, and presidents and politicians came to pray on important Islamic occasions. This was because it possessed one of the holiest relics of the Moslem faith, the head of Husayn, son of Fatimah, Muhammed's daughter. Husayn had been killed in 680 A.D. at the battle of Karbala, a battle fought over the rightful succession to the Caliphate (the leadership of

Islam). It was the supporters of Ali (Husayn's father) and his descendants as Caliph that caused the first major rift in Islam, resulting in the sect known as Shi'ite - Shiah-i-Ali, meaning Partisans of Ali. When Husayn was killed fighting the Sunnis for the right to his succession as Caliph, he became a martyr and, because he was Muhammed's grandson, the El-Husayn Mosque, which holds the sacred relic of his head, draws both Sunnis and Shi'ites alike.

Our minibus nosed its way down a narrow side street and, like a snow-plough, forced pedestrians, barrows, bundles on backs, and children to left and right into doorways. We finally emerged into Midan el-Husayn, a large open square. To one side was a police van – not a Black, nor a Green Maria, but this time a Blue one – outside which a few armed police lounged. We drew up alongside small shops and cafés. The Khan el-Khalili district is famed for its bazaars but at this time of morning steel shutters were still down before the arcades.

The mosque dominated one side of the square. Before we were let loose from the minibus we could hear, from some distant alleyway, a woman's high and shrill demented screaming. We watched as two black clad Arab women came into the square, one of them holding the arm of the other who had obviously lost it completely. Her head was back, her eyes were closed, her mouth deranged, as she shrieked at the top of her voice. The two passed us and walked in the direction of the mosque.

Ali let us out and accompanied us to the great building. It was not the most impressive looking mosque but had been built in 1870 on the site of an earlier twelfth century one. As we crossed the square I noticed a woman with thick curly, unkempt hennaed hair, who had a massive bruise up the side of her face. I lost sight of her as Ali led the way past tall pillars, the top half of which looked like huge furled umbrellas which either opened up as awnings in mid-summer or were purely decorative. We could hear the demented woman screaming the far side of the mosque. The screaming was unremitting and relentless.

The mosque itself was built rather like a fortress-come-palace, with a crenellated roof and single minaret bristling with loud-speakers. Rectangular doorways with above them sculpted arched windows, were its only visible features.

"Do you know what I mean by the Kiswah?" I asked Ali.

"Of course," he replied.

"Is it still woven here in Cairo?" The Kiswah was a gold and black embroidered cloth which was used to cover the Ka'bah, the central shrine at Mecca. I understood that a new Kiswah was woven and embroidered in Cairo every year by men, and I'd wondered whether it was possible to see the men at work on it. The custom had been for camels in full regalia to carry the Kiswah annually from Egypt to Mecca, accompanied by banners, pipes and drums. The sight must have been spectacular.

Ali looked at me politely; it was clear that my reading matter was way out of date. The Kiswah was no longer made in Cairo, he said, but was now manufactured in a factory in Saudi Arabia. A small spark of an ancient custom had gone out.

"But is it still cut up and its pieces sold to Moslems?" I asked.

"Of course. The people feel themselves close to Allah when they have a small piece in their homes." In an odd sort of way I myself would have liked a piece of the cloth. I could imagine Harry pouring scorn on it if I ever brought a piece home with me. For an atheist, he would tell me, I had an extraordinary way of showing it.

One of the legends of the Moslem faith was that a man named Umar (who became the second Caliph) had only been converted to the Moslem faith after he'd hidden under the cloth covering the Ka'bah, where he had overheard Muhammed reciting the Koran. Umar had been an authority on poetry and was immediately spellbound by the nobility and beauty of the verses he was hearing and was instantly converted. It was when Umar was Caliph that Jerusalem fell to the Moslems in 638. The Arab conquests in the seventh century were wide-sweeping and swift.

Ali seemed to have no doubt that I could enter the mosque and my spirits soared because I'd read that the mosque was considered so sacred that no non-Moslem was allowed inside. Before the trip I'd visited the Egyptian Tourist Office in London and had asked about admittance, but had been firmly told by an amiable Egyptian that it was impossible. I liked the man and had argued that nothing was impossible and, surely, I could dress up as a Moslem woman and go in? As he was of a kindly disposition and could see it was as well to humour me, he conceded that of course I could do that but to be sure, if asked, to give a Moslem name like, say, Natasha or Nadine. When I informed Harry of what I'd been told, he'd been highly dismissive. As I wasn't a Moslem, didn't look anything like one, wouldn't know how to behave as one, then I could forget it or he wouldn't come to Egypt at all, so there.

Ali led me to the women's entrance. The screaming woman and her companion had gone to the limits of the square and they were on their way back; the shrilling was as loud as ever. They passed by us as Ali approached the man in a white tarbush standing guard at the women's entrance to the mosque. He spoke to him for a while and I looked beyond into the dark and could only see a brightly illuminated hanging chandelier. The rugged face of the tarbush character looked angry as he glanced in my direction, and Ali came sadly back to inform me what I knew already, that entry was forbidden.

We returned to our vehicle in the wake of the demented woman and her companion. Meanwhile, a small fracas was developing near the shops and cafés. The policemen had stopped lounging and were on the move. Beside our minibus I saw a policeman suddenly seize the hennaed hair of the woman with the massive bruise and drag her away. We were glad when we were back in our minibus with the door shut on the outside world. Inside we felt absurdly secure and safe against the mayhem which humans could unleash on each other. The shrill screaming from the unhinged woman grew fainter as her black clad figure and that of her companion disappeared back down their alleyway.

"What do you think was happening to the woman with the bruised face?" I asked.

"The poor girl's probably been having it off with some fellow," said the Brig easily. "Not done in the Arab world."

"Thank God I didn't let you come for that festival you wanted to see." Harry remarked.

"What festival was that?" asked the Brig's wife.

"The Eid el Adha."

"The Eid el what?"

"It's a celebration of Abraham's willingness to submit to the will of Allah and sacrifice his son, Ishmael."

"I thought it was Isaac?" said the Brig.

"Not for Moslems. For Moslems it's Ishmael."

"Trust the buggers to get it wrong."

"Darling - "

"It's all right, they wouldn't know the word."

"Well, we know the word."

"So tell us about Ishmael," went on the Brig, happily unperturbed. "Keep us awake while we get to the airport."

I told them how Ishmael had been Abraham's son by Hagar, an Egyptian woman who was handmaid to Abraham's wife Sarah. As Sarah was ninety years old and very unlikely to conceive, she'd told Abraham to take Hagar, which he promptly did and she bore a son, Ishmael. For some inexplicable reason God then decided Sarah should also have a son.

"Good heavens! Wouldn't want you in the family way at ninety, old girl! How old was Abraham?"

"A hundred."

"Which is why it was a miracle, darling. Listen to the story."

"Well, once Isaac was born," I continued, "Sarah resented having Hagar and her son around and told Abraham to get rid of them both. Abraham then took them on a long journey down to the Bekkah valley which is where Mecca is. There he trusted in God's mercy and left them in the desert with dates and some water. When their water ran out and the dates were finished, the baby Ishmael cried miserably and started drumming with his heels in the sand."

"Hm. Not surprised, poor blighter." The Brig's wife handed him a cardboard box containing his breakfast which had been packed for us by the hotel. "Ah! Grub! I thought I was beginning to feel peckish."

"So what happened next?" asked the Brig's wife.

"The drumming of Ishmael's heels caused water to gush up from the desert."

"Huh! Another miracle! Then what happened? They couldn't live on water, could they?"

"Well, a few days later some nomads saw birds circling in the distance and, realizing that this must mean water, they went and investigated, found Hagar and Ishmael and that was how Mecca was founded."

"So what was the festival you didn't come to? The Eid el something?"

"The festival that celebrates Abraham's willingness to sacrifice Ishmael to God."

"Oh, that. Yes, I remember."

"Then, when Abraham had the knife poised at Ishmael's throat, God relented and sent a ram to be sacrificed instead."

"Amazing. Can you imagine your reaction, old girl, if I stood over you with a knife and told you that God had told me to kill you? What on earth would you think?"

"I wouldn't expect a ram to appear," was the reply.

"You wouldn't have faith in God?"

"Well, I wouldn't just lie there, darling."

"I should jolly well hope not. I'd hope you'd dial 999 and see I got a bit of counselling."

I really regretted not having come to the Eid el Adha as there would have been whirling dervishes and other ecstatics with skewers through their cheeks, as well as flame swallowers. During this time Moslems slit the throats of newly fattened sheep to share out with family and friends, all of which Harry would have hated. But the reason why I hadn't kept on with the idea was because at the back of my mind the thought of terrorism was firmly rooted. I'd no wish to be one of their sacrificial sheep with my throat cut. One of the hotbeds of fundamentalism was the Al-Azhar University a few hundred yards from the El-Husayn mosque where we'd just been. At least Harry and I had so far remained unscathed with no massive bruising, no police dragging us by the hair, or me shrieking witlessly to the skies. I'd seen most of what I'd wanted to in Cairo and was very happy with that. Now I was looking forward to three days cruising on the Nile. That couldn't be bad.

TEMPLES & CRUISING

THE NILE

We sat on the upper deck of the cruise boat watching the golden shades of the desert, and the fringe of palm trees on the river bank in the evening light. Feluccas, with their tall triangular sails of russet red or ivory white, glided by on their way to somewhere, leaving rippling wakes on the silent, leaden waters. A wild duck skimmed the river and landed amongst reeds on a sandbank.

We sailed past a mud village built up the side of a high hill topped by a monument, probably a tomb, which was catching the last light. The sun, a large red ball, was sinking rapidly; it peeped briefly above the desert horizon and was gone leaving the sky violet. I'd read that the west bank of the Nile was where the dead were buried; the east bank was for the living. We were in the middle, neither dead nor completely alive, but watching.

It was wonderfully relaxing and I was deliberately idling, not because I wanted to but because I needed to, if I was to see any of the great temples of Upper Egypt. I was annoyed with myself for being mortal and taking to my cabin as soon as we'd arrived on board. I'd very much wanted to keep going in order to see the temple of Isis at Philae that afternoon, but our pre-dawn rise in Alexandria, our long drive to Cairo, then our flight to Aswan had left me feeling suddenly icy cold and completely whacked, with the suspicion of a sore throat.

A plan I'd had of trekking off to see a desert monastery, the Monastery of St. Simeon which needed to be approached by camel, lay in tatters. I'd thought it could be arranged whilst everyone else was visiting the Aswan Dam. But the latter had been tied in with the Isis temple and (as Harry was keen to remind me) I couldn't do everything. In fact, at that time I couldn't do anything and didn't care. St. Simeon (of whom little is known) had been in the habit of reading the Bible with his beard tied to the ceiling to stop him from sleeping. 'So what?' was all I could think of in my present condition.

Harry was delighted with my sudden state of inactivity and joined in the lounging with enthusiasm. To do nothing was his idea of the ideal holiday and, after the intense activity of the last few days, he was at last able to indulge himself in total inertia.

There was always something to look at on the Nile. Harry had brought binoculars and we'd seen heron and kingfishers between spells of lazing in a contented, stupefied way. Occasionally, a cruise boat passed going up the Nile and greetings were exchanged. The first sounded its siren in a continuous up-down-up-down blast, and the second responded with short answering trills. We were sailing down the Nile from Aswan. It was difficult getting used to this standing on one's head way of thinking. Upper Egypt was down south on the map and Lower Egypt was up north. The Nile flowed up the map for over six thousand kilometers which seemed impossible.

The aerial view of the Nile, as we'd flown over it from Cairo, had been of endless desert in full sunlight, varied by either sand-drifts, hills or mountain ranges. The sky had been a deep blue with the occasional puff of white cloud casting a dark shadow down below. Canals branched from the great meandering river like fish bones with many hair-like irrigation channels watering patches of cultivation. We'd flown over the pronounced loop of the Nile which I'd thought must be where Nag Hammadi was - where the Gnostic Gospels had been found in one of the many caves.

"What are you reading?" Harry asked suddenly, picking up a book on Egypt which I had lying beside me.

"I'm not." I was attempting to prepare myself for the following day's trip, but felt brainless.

"What temples are we seeing?"

"Can't remember."

"So you don't know where we're going?"

"Not really."

"That's not like you."

"No."

"Group! Follow me, please!" We were at the ancient temple of Edfu. Our tour guide was a round faced, short and solidly built young man in his early thirties, wearing baggy khaki trousers and a navy-blue baseball cap. It was the following day and I'd made a miraculous recovery. The sore throat was more or less under control. We were now a group of about thirty from the cruise boat.

"Ladies and gentlemen, I ask you now to look at this column to which I am pointing!" Flick, flick of finger and thumb as he indicated the hieroglyphs, incised and painted around the base. "Here you have the best hieroglyphs with the colours preserved due to their long years under the sand. You think one man is responsible for the decoration of one column? You are wrong! There are many artists and each one does only the hand, or the beard or the falcon's head and so on. Now, ladies and gentlemen! I want you to notice..." And he pointed a torch which produced a red spot on whatever it was we had to pay special attention to. He had a strong wrist action when he flicked finger and thumb in order to draw our attention to head-dresses, arms, offerings, ankhs and things of paramount importance. "Ladies and gentlemen! I know you like to take photographs and I give you five minutes before we meet back here."

Dark skinned individuals in robes and white turbans lurked around the great columns hoping to be captured on camera before asking for baksheesh. They were darker skinned than in Cairo and had an air of regality about them.

"Group!" We were led on to further halls and chambers which became progressively smaller. He informed us of the ancient New Year festival when all Egypt had celebrated the birth of Horus, the son of the god Osiris and Isis (whose temple I hadn't seen the day before). At this festival his statue would be taken on a litter made of wood borne on the shoulders of a number of priests.

Flick, flick! and our guide pointed to the scene carved on a column. "And ladies and gentlemen, how many priests do you see?" We were all kept on our toes by his questions, but our answers were always wrong. "And why are you wrong? Because, ladies and gentlemen, you see these repeated outlines of the priests. These indicate that there are three, four times as many priests as the one in the foreground. Now, ladies and gentlemen!" Flick,

flick! "You know now that Horus is indicated with the falcon head. We have seen the large granite falcons at the entrance to his temple, now I want you to look up to note the capitals on these columns. They combine the lotus and the papyrus which, ladies and gentlemen, is the plan of Alexander the Great to combine the Hellenistic with the Egyptian religions."

"When was it built?" asked a voice.

"It was first begun 237 B.C. by Ptolemy III Evergetes."

"Oh, so it's not old."

"It's old enough!" He gave a small proud smile. "But you are right, there was first a shrine at the time of Thutmose III who was Pharaoh 1479-1425 B.C. We go on. Group!" The stocky, baggy-trousered figure marched on between the tall columns, an unmistakable figure adept at weaving his way through the other tour groups. He always knew his destination and would stand like a victorious general occupying a newly conquered bit of territory. "Group!" He stood, smiling patiently under his baseball cap. "Group!" He had spotted one of his flock straying.

With us all assembled, he began with as much energy as at the start. "Ladies and gentlemen! Here we are now in the Sacrarium! What is the Sacrarium? It is where the image of the god was housed."

And we were told how the god was taken daily from his sanctuary and up a corridor to see the sun where he would renew his energy before being returned to his throne (not entirely unlike my renewal of energy in the late afternoon sun the day before). A hefty granite block for sacrifice stood before the throne. Under the watchful eye of the priests people would bring animals and birds for sacrifice, the best parts being offered to Horus before being discreetly gobbled up by the priests.

We left the inner sanctum to allow another gathering to enter. "Group!" We followed the waving arm as the sturdy figure in the baseball cap marched on. Eventually we were stopped before a long wall covered with hieroglyphs depicting religious scenes which included the cult of Horus, his birth and his victory over his father's enemies.

Our guide studied us all as we gathered around. Satisfied that we were all there, he began with his usual call for our attention: "Ladies and gentlemen! I want now to tell you our Egyptian version of your Romeo and Juliet story." Flick, flick. "Here you have the god Osiris and here his wife Isis." He pointed to hieroglyphs and cartouches, all of which by now we were supposed to identify and understand. "Can one of you please come forward and stand by me? One of you, please! Sir!" He selected an elderly grey-head. "Sir! I want you now to choose your Isis. Where is your beautiful Isis?" Osiris looked self-consciously around. "Where's my wife?" he mumbled.

"Sir! it doesn't have to be your wife! You are free to choose anybody!" He gave a conspiratorial smile.

"It'd better be my wife, or I'll be in trouble."

Our tour guide nodded understandingly. A grey-headed woman came forward looking well satisfied.

"Good! So now we have Isis. Now, another man, please!" Realizing he was dealing with British citizens who were unlikely to volunteer, he selected a tall middle-aged man to stand beside Osiris. This was Seth, Osiris' evil brother. Soon another woman, a beauty in her thirties, was chosen to be Isis' sister, Nephetys.

"Now, ladies and gentlemen, we have here Osiris, his beautiful wife, Isis - please, madam, play your part and show you love each other!" Isis flung her arms around her husband's neck. "And his brother Seth and Isis' sister, Nephetys. Ladies and gentlemen, Osiris represents all that is good and his brother all that is bad. Now, ladies and gentlemen!" Flick flick, and our attention was drawn to several figures carved on the wall. "The wicked Seth is jealous of his brother because he has a beautiful wife." The elderly wife fluttered her eyelashes and her husband played to the gallery with expressions of mock despair. "So what does the wicked Seth do? He gives a large party. Before the party he makes a beautiful casket which he knows fits Osiris exactly. Ladies and gentlemen, all his guests are also his accomplices, so it is no surprise that during the party he arranges that the guests all play the game of seeing who fits exactly into this casket, because whoever does will, he promises, be presented with it as a gift. So what happens? Ladies and gentlemen, as soon as Osiris lies down in the casket which fits him perfectly, the lid is put down on him and he is locked inside and thrown into the River Nile. There are variations to the story but let me give you this one. I want one more gentleman, please. You, please!" The Brig was hauled out and made to stand with the others. "You, sir, are Ra, the sun-god. As the sun-god, Ra, you breathe new life into the dead Osiris because, believe me, Osiris is very dead in this beautiful casket. Somehow he comes out of his casket and, don't ask me how he comes out, but he is given the kiss of life by Ra."

"I'm not giving him the kiss of anything," growled the Brig.

"And Seth, ladies and gentlemen! Seth, he is so angry that he has Osiris cut up in many pieces and he hides the pieces all over Egypt. So what about Isis? Poor Isis, she is distraught and searches for the pieces of her beloved Osiris. There are fourteen pieces and she gets thirteen of them, but there is one vital piece missing. Can you guess what the one vital piece missing from her husband can be?" The conspiratorial smile threatened to become broader. "Ladies and gentlemen! I will not name it but let us for politeness sake say it is his wallet!" He paused to make sure we were enjoying the joke before continuing cheerfully: "Without his wallet poor Osiris is in a plight, and the sun-god, Ra, takes pity and allows Osiris to have his wallet for one day - perhaps it is five minutes - but it is for long enough. Because - yes, you've guessed it! - thanks to having his wallet for those five minutes, nine months later Horus is born!" Flick, flick! and our attention was drawn to the falcon-headed offspring depicted on the wall.

"So, ladies and gentlemen, we have the divine triad. It is Horus who combats with his wicked uncle Seth to avenge his father's murder. And also, ladies and gentlemen, you have to remember this! It is Horus who is believed in ancient times to defend and protect the reigning Pharaoh. The Pharaoh is the god Horus and his mother is the divine Isis! And, when the Pharoah dies, he becomes Osiris and his successor then becomes Horus. In this way the gods and the rulers are honoured because they have the power to bring prosperity to the people. All the stories of Osiris, Isis and Horus are here on the walls and columns of this great temple. Do you like this temple at Edfu?" The lively eyes under the baseball cap searched the beginning-to-flag faces of his audience. "You can ask yourselves how do they build it, or why do they build it, or a hundred other questions, but I think you will agree, ladies and gentlemen, it is built to impress all those who come to see it." He glanced at his watch. "Ladies and gentlemen, I give you half an hour to take your photographs and we meet outside by the caleches."

Harry and I wandered like ants amongst the massive columns and made our way through the progressively smaller rooms to the inner sanctuary.

"I can't think why they built these temples so large," I said. "If they were half the size they'd still be impressive. They're totally over the top."

"Perhaps it was just a way of keeping Joe public occupied chiselling away or painting hieroglyphs."

"Can you imagine all this in the name of religion?"

"Why not? The Pharaoh, alias the god Haw-Haw or whoever, had to do something to inspire his subjects."

We left the precinct of shady columns and gigantic walls and made our way across the vast shadeless approach to the outer road where there was a bazaar.

We joined the Brig and his wife haggling over embroidered table-cloths. I was interested in a colourful rug but the vendor began unfolding all his rugs. "Madame! Madame! Look, I show you! You buy two? Look, madame! I make it cheap!" I wanted to look and to examine, but there was no let-up as the vendor threw all his wares at my feet, most of which I didn't want. I would have liked to have pondered over colourful kaftans hanging on a rail, but didn't dare look at them. In the end I settled for one of the rugs which would make a good throw-over for a threadbare armchair.

We pressed on through the bazaar, ignoring all the wares for fear of catching anybody's eye. Children in tattered garments approached hopefully, selling beads. Our caleches (horse-drawn carriages with leather hoods) were lined up waiting to take us back to our boat. Ours was number seven hundred with a tall dark-skinned half negroid driver in a long white garment. His caleche was clean and his horse well fed and groomed. We'd been told by our guide that if a horse, donkey or mule, or a member of the family needed medical attention, then the animal got priority because the family's livelihood depended on it.

Our driver tried to whine to the Brig, showing him his finger and hoping for a little baksheesh. Apparently the Brig had accidentally stood on it as he'd climbed into the caleche on our trip from the boat.

"Finger no good," said the driver.

"Finger very good!" said the Brig looking at it briefly. "Nothing wrong with your finger. Very good finger!" The Brig heaved himself up and sat heavily down in his corner.

"You good man. Number one man," said the driver hoping to get baksheesh by flattery.

"You've got it right, old chap. I number one man, you number seven hundred." And he cheerfully made several dismissive remarks which satisfied the driver that he, number seven hundred, was decidely superior to number one.

We set off at a smart trot, the caleche swaying in a bone-shaking way. The Brig sat solidly in his corner on the torn, black leather seat, hanging onto the side and muttering something about wanting to get out to take a taxi - of feeling seasick - of long odds against us coming to the boat before number three hundred who was trotting alongside. The driver used his whip to keep things moving and sang at the top of his voice. The song was black African and very different to Arab music.

The Brig's wife said: "I'm glad to see their horses are in good condition."

"Their horses are their livelihood, old girl. They'll let their wives and children go to pot before their livestock."

"That's dreadful."

"Oh, I don't know. A wife knows her place. I know my place where your horses are concerned. I'm only the groom and the mucker out of stables." He looked quite happy about it.

His wife, with her wild grey hair and bright blue eyes, surveyed the trotting horses and swaying caleches and remarked: "That one over there is going lame."

"You don't have to worry about that," the Brig remarked. "It'll get veterinary treatment. It's if the wife goes lame that you have to worry."

When we reached the area where cruise boats were moored side by side and three deep, we were immediately accosted by more ragged, wide-eyed children selling beads and shawls. There was one ten year old sitting on a donkey whipping his beast and making it cavort and buck or go at a canter up and down the road; he was either practising his skill at staying seated on its back, or training the donkey to his will, or just performing antics to impress us.

Leaving the clamouring children and the caleches with their colourful trappings, we walked along a gang-plank to the cruise boats, and escaped from the noise and bustle of the bazaar, passing through the security checks of the first vessel, then to the next boat and on to our own. I was conscious of the elitism of our existence, and felt ashamed at how very pleased I was with it.

The next morning we woke early. We'd been told that at six we would pass through one of the great barrier locks on the Nile. Idly I turned on the television in our cabin and pressed the channel which showed the prow of our boat and our progress down the Nile. In fact, it revealed that we were still stationary. A line of concrete pylons the width of the river made up the barrage and the lock gates were still closed. The occasional headlights of a car crossing the river over the barrage could be seen.

I pulled back the curtains to the picture windows of our cabin and looked out at the Nile in its still dark early morning tranquility. Towards the horizon the sky looked as though a city was burning. The black silhouette of the far bank was a long dark outline with groups of palm trees rising here and there and all of it reflected in the Nile waters, sky and silhouettes together.

I poked my head out of the window and saw the massive lock gates with traffic still passing over them. Harry came and joined me and we watched a long barge laden with huge rocks sailing past to take up its position infront of us. The wheel of the barge was like a cart-wheel but with fine spokes.

We suddenly saw a break appear in the lock gates and two speeding cyclists just making it before the gap became too wide. Soon the gates were fully open and the water stretched beyond ready for boats to pass through.

The long width of the Nile barrage with its solid concrete pylons were by now bathed in a soft pink light. Another barge sailed past; it was lying deep in the water weighed down by its heavy cargo of rocks.

We drew alongside the massive concrete tow path to the open lock gates where hawkers were already waiting with rugs, shawls and things that those on cruise boats might like to buy to take home as souvenirs. "Madame! Madame! Hello! Hello! How are you? Madame, very cheap! You buy!" I saw a young fellow holding up a rug I very much liked but I automatically withdrew. I could hear the hawkers go the length of the boat, shouting: "Hello!

How are you? Madame! Madame!"

The sun was soon fully above the horizon casting a brilliant path like a shimmering cloak on the blue-grey of the Nile waters. Magical colours in shades of gold spread across the distant desert sand.

We began moving. Once beyond the barrage we were again able to watch the Nile scene: some water-buffalo standing by the river bank; a donkey standing docile, ears drooping contentedly as it was ferried across in a rowing-boat; a riverside estate with a grove of palm trees; hills, mountains, desert - it was all quietly hypnotic.

We stood bemused trying to be intelligent about more colossal columns. We were now at Luxor and I was wanting to understand the ancient Egyptian mentality. Why had there been this desire for over-the-top enormousness in everything? In Greece the temples had been elegant, and in keeping with the landscape; they both stood out and merged with their environment. Here in Egypt the Pharaoh was making a statement of some sort; there was not so much a call to worship as a call to subject yourself. Yes, it was impressive but it didn't touch the soul with its grandeur, it belittled and clobbered the human mind.

We had our same tour guide in his baseball cap and baggy trousers. We were flick-flicked from hieroglyph to hieroglyph, and martialled and summoned to the call of 'Group!'

The temple at Luxor was founded in the reign of Amenhotep III (1390-1352 B.C.) and enlarged by later Pharaohs such as Ramses II and finally Alexander the Great. In ancient Egypt the name of a person, and certainly a Pharaoh, was considered of great importance. It meant as much as his ka (creative life force), his ba (personality), and his akh (the reunion of his ba and ka at his death), and his shadow. These, together with his name, made up the whole person. The name often incorporated the deity of the times or for non-royals a local god. For example Ramses II contained the name Ra, the sun-god. Amenhotep III had in it Amun. The interesting thing about him was that his son Amenhotep IV challenged the ancient beliefs, defied all the old gods and worshipped the Aten (the orb of the sun), changing his name from Amenhotep (Amun is content) to Akhenaten (glory of the sun). He was so obsessed with the Aten that, in the fifth year of his reign, he tried to destroy all evidence of Amun and moved his capital city from Luxor to Middle Egypt (today's El-Amarna) which at the time had been unsullied by any previous worship of Amun. There he built temples dedicated only to the Aten.

Inscriptions of prayers and hymns to the Aten dating from this period have been discovered. One is of particular interest because of its similarity to Psalm 104, suggesting that the Israelites were influenced by Akhenaten's form of monotheism, or he had been by them.

Akhenaten liked to depict himself and his wife, Nefertiti, together with their six daughters, as worshipping the Aten, proffering sceptres as a sign of power and ankhs as a sign of eternal life.

"The fascinating thing," I said to Harry, "is that his successor - at least, I think he was or else he was as near as damn it - was Tutankhamun. And Tutankhamun was actually first called Tutankhaten which means the living image of the Aten."

"You mean he reverted to the worship of Amun?"

"Yes. And he re-decorated the colonnade at Luxor, restoring the name of his ancestor Amenhotep III. Anyway, something of the sort. Quite frankly, what's different amongst all the gods? Amun - Aten - Zeus - Yahweh - God - Allah - the great world spirit - soul - ka - ba - They're all words for the unknown."

We'd arrived at the Luxor temple from Karnak where the original temple complex had been in honour of Amun-Ra, his wife Mut and son Khons (another divine triad). The processional road flanked by sphinxes with human faces stretched for about one and a half miles from Karnak to Luxor. It had been the route taken at the ancient fifteen-day celebration of the Egyption New Year festival of Opet, which was held on the second month of the inundation of the Nile (late August). The festival had been celebrated with a procession of sacred barques carried by thirty priests.

Of greater interest to me was not so much the colossal granite figures of Ramses II at the entrance to the great colonnaded court with its walloping columns, but the fascinating small mosque perched on a higher level bang in the middle of the colonnade. Its crenellated roof, its inky-blue and yellow geometric patterned tiles decorating its entranceway, and its higher glassless arched windows and lower gridded rectangular ones, made it a unique and unexpected feature poised there in this ancient temple precinct. A tall, elegant minaret topped by a round sun (or globe) with above it a crescent moon containing a star, was unusual.

"Ladies and gentlemen! Before we move on I would like to draw your attention to the line you can see on the wall below the mosque. It marks the level of the sand before excavations began here at Luxor. Ladies and gentlemen! Napoleon began a new era for Egypt and in 1811 - What happens in 1811?" After waiting briefly for an answer, he enlightened us. "It was an Englishman, your Thomas Cook - yes! You look surprised! But Thomas Cook he opens the first travel agency in the world and then many people they come to visit Luxor, not as you see it now, but as it was painted by your David Roberts. Ladies and gentlemen! you may not believe this when I tell to you that your Lady Lucy Duff-Gordon lives for seven years in a house built on the roof of the Temple of Amun!" Murmurs of appreciation and surprise. "Much of Luxor is at that time built above on the roofs of these buildings and, with the coming of tourism, these village houses they have to be moved." Flick-flick and our attention was drawn back to the mosque. "Ladies and gentlemen! Why is the mosque there? There is only one reason for it. It is because the people of Luxor will not allow anyone to destroy it. Negotiations even now are taking place to move it to another location, but to many it is sacred because it marks the sepulchre of the local Moslem saint, Abu el-Haggag, who died in 1244 A.D. There is a legend that his body was brought here by angels, and there is a festival held here every year in his honour which is very similar to the ancient New Year festival."

"Can I go up there?"

"Of course, but it is a steep climb to it."

"You don't want to go into the mosque!" said Harry unhelpfully.

"You have to take care climbing the steps," warned our tour guide, preparing to move on. I wavered hopelessly. I would have liked to have gone inside, didn't want to upset the group, and capitulated under Harry's lack of encouragement.

"Group!" The sturdy figure of our guide marched on to an obelisk. "Ladies and gentlemen! We stop here to take a look at this one remaining obelisk with its remarkable reliefs. The obelisk was intended to receive the first rays of the sun. You see the top is shaped like a pyramid? The top it was once gilded in order to reflect the sun's rays. Ladies and gentlemen!" Suddenly the call to prayer from the muezzin drowned him. The call resounded off all the temple walls and circulated in and out of the gigantic columns before bludgeoning our ears: 'Allah is always great. We trust Allah. We trust Muhammed. Praying is good. Come to pray...' Our guide was not at all put out but continued speaking. "Lad.. an.. gen..! Do y.. kn.. wh..th.. are th.. bab.. ar... th.. ba.. o..th.. ob..?" The eyes under the baseball cap regarded us enthusiastically as he pointed to a series of granite baboons around the base of the obelisk. He put a cupped hand to his ear hoping to catch an answer. "I...i.. be... th.. baboons they always jump up and down at sunrise and chatter." His voice suddenly yelled out clearly as the call to prayer ceased.

He waved an arm onwards and we dutifully followed the solid figure marching between columns. He paused beside a doorway and pointed out to me a damaged wall of stone blocks with some hieroglyphs, and a high arched recess flanked by two pillars with corinthian capitals, beside a dark doorway to the inner sanctum. "This is an early church," he told me. "As you are interested I point it out to you. You can see, but not clearly, the frescoes of the Last Supper."

I immediately abandoned the group and examined the faintest traces of the Christian frescoes. Whether they depicted the Last Supper or not was hard to make out. Yet it was a fact that Christians had observed their own beliefs there. Where the plaster had fallen away I could see an ankh being proffered or received, representing the earlier belief of resurrection and eternal life.

I followed the others into the Hall of Offerings, and the inner sanctuary where the barque of Amun had been placed at the time of the Opet Festival. More flick-flicks and pointings to various hieroglyphic scenes of sacrificial cows, before we were marched on to the room of the Divine Birth where the nativity of Amenhotep III was depicted, showing the interaction between gods and human life and destiny.

For example Isis was pictured presenting the child Amenhotep to Amun; and Amenhotep and his ka (creative life force) being watched and cared for by the gods who were presenting the ka to Amun.

The ankh was to be seen everywhere engraved into the granite, reminding the viewer of eternal life.

"Don't you think the ankh is really fascinating and understandable from today's view-point?" I remarked to Harry. "Their belief in resurrection and becoming one with their god is just like we today believe we return to God."

"So now you believe in God?" asked Harry, pointing out that in my usual vacillating way I was swinging in that direction. But the commanding word of 'Group!' summoned us, and prevented me considering the answer to that knotty question.

We forgathered around the baseball cap which was all I could see of our tour guide. "Ladies and gentlemen! You have here very interesting hieroglyphs which show Alexander the Great appearing before the god Amun. And what is he wearing? You are right, madam! He is seen here wearing the clothes of the Egyptian Pharaoh. Ladies and gentlemen! He wears the clothes of a Pharaoh so that the Egyptian people will know he takes his duties towards them seriously. As you know, Alexander the Great preached peace to all countries he conquered!" I had a view of the face under the baseball cap as somebody moved. He had his conspiratorial smile as his lively eyes moved over the line of faces gathered around him. "Alexander the Great never visited Luxor, but it is evident from these scenes carved here, that his power and influence reached to all parts of Egypt. He was not a destroyer but a builder. He invested money in the temples which were important to the people and, in this way, they came to trust him. Now we move on!"

Gradually we completed the circuit of Luxor, from staring at the hieroglyphs on the colonnade, to running three times anti-clockwise for good luck (seven times to get pregnant) around the giant scarab beetle on a pedestal, to admiring the colossal figure of Ramses II with the Mona Lisa smile.

"You'd think the poor chaps had nothing else to do but carve hierglyphs!" commented the Brig as he came alongside with his wife.

"Just to think of raising these columns - to have them up and all the same height! It's extraordinary! Quite extraordinary!"

"Marvellous what you can do if you're determined enough, and have the labour," muttered the Brig.

The clear early morning light on the stark desert mountains with their shadowed folds and crevices was mystical. We had just crossed the Nile, passing from east to west, from life to death, and were heading for the Valley of the Kings. It was over there that Islamic fundamentalists had opened fire on a tour group, killing sixty people at the tomb of Queen Hatshepsut in the Valley of the Queens.

Did the fundamentalists choose this particular tourist attraction for their murderous purpose because of its association with death? We ourselves - a large moving target in a coach - felt extraordinarily unthreatened as we headed for the Valley of the Kings.

Suddenly above the desert scene the sky was brightened by a crimson hot-air balloon floating overhead. The swoosh and roar of flames shot upwards to keep the balloon inflated. A few heads peered over the basket. A short distance away was a striped green and yellow balloon, then a green and purple one. They soared majestically over the mountains and wide valleys, then away.

We passed a solitary impressive domed building perched on a bare hill, and were told it had been the house of Howard Carter during the years he'd been busy excavating the area. He'd been financed by Lord Carnarvon and certainly his home looked as if some millionaire had been involved.

We were put out at the base of the site. A shuttle service of toy-like yellow and blue painted trailers with seats drawn by blue toy-like cabs, chugged slowly up and down the dusty hill to the tomb area. Each burial chamber had been cut into the rock face.

"Another way of keeping the masses out of mischief!" announced the Brig.

The corridor we entered sloped downwards to the burial chamber, and its walls and ceiling were covered with painted hieroglyphs, and script revealing prayers and the deeds and accomplishment of the Pharaoh. No detail was spared, and every corner of the surface of the rock was filled with pigmented colour. There were detailed pictures of the gods and their legends; appeals to Amun, to Ra, to Osiris; hieroglyphs representing the ka, ba, akh; jackal-headed gods, vulture-headed ones, falcon-headed and ram-headed ones; scarabs, snakes, crocodiles, baboons; numerous ankhs. The walls were protected by glass and the colours, which had been sealed off from the light of day and from weather conditions over thousands of years, were still vivid and fresh.

The artisans had their own village on this west bank, in order to be near the tombs where they were employed as scribes and painters. The god Thoth (represented first as a baboon, then as an ibis) was god of knowledge and writing. There was a hymn inscribed on a statue of the Pharaoh Horemheb extolling the god 'whose words last for all time'. Hieroglyphs were considered to be the writing of 'God's words', both sacred and eternal once incised. It represented the interplay between the divine and the mortal, bringing the past forward to the present.

"We don't think enough about the wonders of writing," I said to Harry, "how it conveys meaning and ideas from an unseen hand - I mean from someone unknown to you. Look at all this! It's a message to us today from four thousand years ago! I haven't a clue what it means, but there are people who spend a lifetime working it all out. Isn't that odd? What makes someone inspired and focused enough to want to spend his life trying to unravel hieroglyphs? And don't say money, because that's incidental to having the devotion and enthusiasm in the first place."

"The ba and ka of some ancient recyling itself," said the Brig who was standing behind me. "Never stops coming back, so it's bound to get excited about what it recognizes from the past."

"Darling, you can't really believe that!"

"Can't really believe anything! It's as good an answer as any," he remarked, moving on.

"Look! that's definitely their day of judgement with the weighing of the Pharaoh's heart against the feather of whoever!" I pointed out to Harry.

"Is that Ra, the sun-god?"

"Yes, I think so - with the serpent trying to swallow him." I'd read that serpents were regarded as evil and were believed to threaten the sun when it went down at night and journeyed through the netherworld.

There was too little time and too much to take in. I rapidly lost all idea of which tomb was which, and I became completely bemused, my mind like a tangled ball of wool which, the more I tried to unravel it, the more knotted it became. Not to worry, Harry remarked, when I told him I was sliding into a bog of witlessness.

The discovery of Tutankhamun's tomb had been the jewel in Harold Carter's crown, and is today remembered by a day of celebration to mark the occasion. Its discovery has been well documented, though there were accusations bandied around that there'd been scrolls found by Carter which had never been made public because they contained writings which would 'change the thinking of the world'. It was good secretive stuff, the theory being that the rebel king Akhenaten, first ever monotheist, was none other than Moses who led the Israelites out of Egypt.

Sigmund Freud, a Jew himself, wrote a book entitled Moses and Monotheism, in which he expounded the theory that Moses, who'd given the Israelites their monotheistic laws and religion, had been an aide to Akhenaten. He suggested that, on the death of the Pharaoh, the old Amun priesthood at Luxor (which had been proscribed) got its own back by obliterating all that it could of the Aten worship, and moving the capital city back to Thebes. Freud's theory was that Moses alone remained faithful to the monotheistic

Aten religion, and used the Israelites to fulfil his religious conviction, by promising them their own land.

"Don't suppose it matters who Moses was," Harry remarked, when I told him. "They were still Israelites getting out of Egypt."

"But it's odd that Lord Carnarvon, who financed the whole project, concealed certain writings that would 'change the thinking of the world'," I persisted. "The suspicion was that Carnarvon was sworn to secrecy by the Rothschild family - Carnarvon's in-laws were Rothschild - because, as wealthy Jews, they were deeply involved in the setting up of the new state of Israel. The last thing they wanted was a revelation that they had never been God's chosen people but were chosen by Moses, and their 'promised land' was merely their determination to grab it, using God as their justification for it."

The Brig and his wife came back up the decking which was laid on the uneven ground to prevent tourists from breaking their legs or twisting their ankles. "Must have taken a hundred strong men," he said. "The sarcophagus must be everything of thirty tons."

"We're wondering whether to pay the extra for Tutankhamun's tomb," said his wife.

"Damned waste of money," grumbled the Brig. "Give you a good dinner when we get back instead."

"It's got a curse on it," I said. "People who've gone in die early."

"Probably the poor blighters who got murdered by the terrorists had just been inside."

"Darling, not so loud."

"Hum."

"Group!"

We were summoned to continue our journey.

"Death on the Nile!" declared the Brig. "That's just the book to bring out to Egypt!"

One or two Egyptian-looking individuals glanced at the Brig who, with his gusto and good humour, seemed impervious to the idea that his remark might seem inappropriate. We were in the departure lounge at Cairo airport waiting to be called. It was mid-afternoon and there we were, having only that morning been in the Valley of the Kings and the Valley of the Queens. Soon we would be in London.

I already had a plan for the next trip. I'd read of a tour that took people into the Sinai. It entailed trekking on camels and meeting the Bedouin. The highlight of it would be several nights in St. Catherine's Monastery which marked the spot where Moses was said to have heard God speaking from a burning bush. I was already looking forward to the following year.

BETWEEN MECCA & JERUSALEM

5

SINAI

We were at peace with the world as we sat out on the balcony of our five star luxury hotel. For reasons known only to our tour operator we'd been upgraded from a more modest hotel to this five star luxury at no extra cost. I wondered whether it was in order to have all foreigners under one roof in case they had to be got out of the country quickly.

During the previous months there'd been ever increasing media hype regarding war with Iraq and Islamic terrorism. Several weeks before departure I'd rung the Brig and his wife to get their views. "Not go on hols?" queried the Brig, "I don't suppose Saddam Hussein will want to target us. Unless the F.O. advises against it we're on our way. Can't stop us." His words lifted us immediately from we-shouldn't-risk-it thoughts to renewed enthusiasm.

As we'd flown over the Sinai peninsular we'd looked down at the wild terrain with its upward thrust of ginger-brown sandstone crags and mountains. The late afternoon sun had thrown golden light and shadow over this remarkable, wind-torn and barren landscape. Ravines and valleys were marked by drifts of pale desert sand. The thought that we'd soon be travelling through this wilderness filled me with a surge of excitement.

From where we now lazed on our balcony we overlooked a magnificent landscaped garden of colourful flower-beds, palm trees, and meandering tarmac pathways leading to a complex of swimming-pools. Beyond it lay the Gulf of Aqaba and the Red Sea. The sun was warm and the sky was blue, as was to be expected for the end of February in Egypt. Bougainvillaea clambered and trailed over walls and balconies in vivid hues of pink, mauve and cream. I heard the musical up-and-down-an-octave call of an egret before I caught sight of its ivory-coloured plumage. It was the shape and size of a guinea-fowl and strutted between palm trees and shrubs, elongating and drawing back its head with every step.

Looking across the Red Sea I supposed I was sitting at a triangular point roughly equidistant between the two most holy cities of the world. To gaze towards the south-east was to look in the direction of Mecca, and to turn to the north-east was to look towards Jerusalem.

I began thumbing through a hotel Bible which I'd found placed in a drawer beside the bed. I thought it odd to find an English Bible, not a Koran. I found the Book of Exodus and began skimming through the chapters searching for the passage about Moses leading the Israelites across the Red Sea.

"It's really odd how God suddenly whizzed around and made himself known to Moses in a burning bush on Sinai and then later to Muhammed in Mecca," I commented. Harry was following the movements of the egret with his binoculars. "It caused God so much bother. Have I told you that, according to various books I've read, Allah was not new to Mecca, but was one amongst many other gods? He was al-Lah, meaning 'the god', and had three daughters. He was, I think, the chief god and there were three hundred and sixty others worshipped at the Ka'bah."

"Do you want to look? It's a really comical bird with a round beady eye." Harry was transfixed by the egret.

"The point being that even God admitted there were other gods which is why he was so insistent that he alone was to be worshipped," I went on. " 'No other God but me' sort of command. As for the Ka'bah itself - and this, I think, is really interesting! - it had always been considered sacred with an area around it where people sought sanctuary. Long before Muhammed, there existed an annual hajj or pilgrimage to it, and there was the custom of circumambulating seven times around it. Muhammed merely absorbed into Islam pagan customs that were already there."

"There go the Brig and his wife heading for the pool." Harry trained the binoculars from the egret to the military figure ambling along with his wife who paused to admire a flower-bed. He was clearly more interested in seeing the obvious than speculating on the unseen.

"What am I looking at, the Gulf of Aqaba or the Red Sea?" Harry was now peering through the binoculars out to sea.

"Sort of both, I think. The one goes into the other," I replied. "I'd like to take a trip down the Red Sea," I added. "I'd really like to go to Jedda and get as close to Mecca as possible."

"Well, I don't think you want to be the only white woman amongst a lot of fanatical Moslems heading for Mecca. Particularly at this time."

"In that case I'd just like to be on the Red Sea because of the Israelites crossing it. It's why the Jews have their annual Passover - or do they celebrate it because God 'passed over' the marked doors of the Israelites in order to kill only the Egyptian first-born? I've forgotten which it is, but really! God in his wrath destroyed thousands of people - thousands! Probably millions! I mean, talk of terrorism! Take Exodus for a start! There God murdered all the first-born of the Egyptians to get his Israelites out of Egypt. And he didn't think twice either of annihilating his own 'stiff-necked', 'chosen people', whenever they displeased him. If God were human he'd have been tried and condemned centuries ago. I wouldn't think it even good for God to have such power if he chooses to use it destructively every time he's crossed!"

"If you want my opinion, which I don't suppose you do, I think it's important to put your faith in a caring God, or you'll go mad."

"So it's all psychological?"

"It's all a question of keeping a right perspective in the wider pattern of things. And if you want another opinion, I think that for one who's trying to act the atheist, you have an incredible way of playing the part. There you are with a Bible in one hand and endlessly talking about God who, in your view, doesn't exist!"

"Oh. Well. Yes, I suppose you're right."

I fell silent and thought instead about the Prophet Muhammed. As a young man in Mecca, Muhammed had been illiterate, but had learned about monotheism from Jewish and Christian merchants who'd passed along the Arabian trade routes to Mecca. After ten years of enlightenment, which put him increasingly in conflict with the local tribes of Mecca worshipping their idols, Muhammed and his devotees moved two hundred miles north to Medina where there were many settled Jews.

There he learned more about the Jewish prophets, and Jewish beliefs and disciplines.

Before turning towards Mecca Muhammed had first prayed to Al-lah (the God) facing towards Jerusalem like the Jews did; he also had regular prayer meetings on Fridays, the evening of which was the start of the Jewish Sabbath.

Learning how the Jews traced their lineage to Abraham through his son Isaac, Muhammed was further enlightened to declare he and his followers were descended from Abraham by way of Abraham's first-born, Ishmael. Moslems, like Christians, soon found a passage in Isaiah foretelling the coming of Muhammed: 'Behold my servant, whom I uphold, my chosen, in whom my soul delights; I have put my Spirit upon him, he will bring forth justice to the nations...' (Isaiah 42:1-5)

It was at Medina that Muhammed began to celebrate the Jewish Yom Kippur festival held in the month of Tishri. The tenth day of Tishri is the Jewish Day of Atonement, when Jews remember the offence of their forebears who worshipped the golden calf whilst Moses was receiving the ten commandments.

But, in time, the tenth day of Tishri became known to the Moslems as 'Ashura' which is 'tenth' in Arabic. Today the Moslem 'Ashura' is held annually on the tenth day, not of Tishri, but of the Moslem month of Muharram, the first day of which is the Moslem New Year which celebrates Muhammed's first arrival at Medina. Any dating of Islamic events are reckoned from this time. But, whilst Yom Kippur is always in the autumn for the Jews, Muharram for Moslems falls eleven days earlier every year because their calendar is lunar. Our trip that year was, in fact, coinciding with the Moslem New Year on the 4th March.

In a few days there would be a crescent moon signalling the start of it.

Harry put away the binoculars. "Definitely hot enough to bathe. Shall we go to the pool now?" he suggested.

We left the peace of our balcony to prepare ourselves for a swim. Whilst I attired myself in a bathing-suit with suitable covering garments to go out without offending Moslem eyes, Harry turned on the television World Service news. An Iraqi spokesman was being interviewed, and was arguing that it was unreasonable for Iraq to be told to get rid of newly discovered missiles or else face war, because it was obvious that America intended to invade Iraq anyway, and the weapons would be needed for the country's defence. As for chemical and biological weapons, how could Iraq destroy them, or the U.N. weapon inspectors find them, when Iraq hadn't got any?

Weapons or no weapons - smoking gun, or no smoking gun - I was looking forward to the following day when we would be travelling into the Sinai desert. It was clearly better not to watch the news with all this talk of war. For the present moment a peaceful swim, or a restful lounge, was something to be enjoyed after all the stress of preparing for and embarking on this journey.

"What are those chaps doing staring out at the desert?" asked the Brig as we left the suburbs of Sharm el-Sheikh and drove along a flat, straight tarmac road heading for the Sinai hills. Every hundred yards an armed policeman on either side of the road stood with his back to the traffic, staring across the flat desert terrain to the horizon. A few gazed with an air of boredom at their boots.

"It is because of the Arab summit which takes place now in Sharm el-Sheikh," explained Zayeed, our guide. He was a young man with a solid round face and pleasant smile. He turned his head around from where he sat beside the driver. We were in a Land Rover which had seats along the sides. It was a rattly affair but had good new tyres - something I'd noted as it had squealed to a stop outside our impressive hotel entrance. The receptionist had looked shocked when I'd told him we were abandoning his five star comfort for three days in the desert. I was afraid the hotel might forbid it for security reasons, except I supposed as adults we were free to do as we chose. From being under the umbrella of one package tour, we were entrusting ourselves to three days organized by another company which specialized in the Sinai and provided a guide and four-wheel drive.

Harry, who never speaks to foreigners except in matters of extreme emergency, asked me to ask Zayeed if he knew what the results were of the Arab summit. I hesitated regarding such a sensitive subject. The Brig, who'd heard Harry's request, jumped in with the question. "What's the news, Zayeed? Are they coming up with a solution about the Iraqi problem?"

"Excuse me?"

"We haven't any ruddy newspapers and we're wondering what the Arab summit's come up with?"

"There is no news yet," came the pleasant answer.

"Probably all drinking?" enquired the Brig cheerfully.

"Darling!" rebuked his wife.

Zayeed, whose head was wrapped in an Arab red and white check keffiyeh, continued to smile in a relaxed, enigmatic way. But the Brig was enjoying his 'hols', as he put it, and was unstoppable. "Bad thing all this talk of war," he grumbled loudly. "We ourselves are all against it, Zayeed. Better things to do with our time. Haven't planted my shallots yet, for a start."

Zayeed knew better than to take up the cudgels of speech and held his peace, smiling pleasantly and staring out at the desert which reached to a horizon of opaque sky which, in its turn merged to azure, and then a deep blue in the heavens. It was only 9 a.m.

"Good road!" declared the Brig after a while.

"Yes. It is built by the Israelis," explained Zayeed.

"That's something good you got out of them! The October War, was it? Yom Kippur War and all that?" asked the Brig, grasping hold of something to keep himself from falling off his seat. "You beat them then, didn't you, Zayeed? Got them out of their settlements they'd built up here in the Sinai after their 1967 Six Day War?" As an aside to us behind his hand he hissed, "Actually part of peace negotiations which took years!"

Zayeed continued to smile patiently. He was probably trying to assess us, his new group, with whom he was going to have to spend the next few days.

Our driver, Abdullah, was a lean figure in Arab dress and jacket. He had a dark, gaunt face and eyes like burning coals. He had a way of squaring his shoulders when driving at speed and leaning his body to left or right as he took the bends in the road. We left the flat desert behind and began to climb, cutting through the rugged mountainous landscape.

We drove through biblical territory, said to be where the Israelites had wandered forty years in the wilderness, though quite why it had taken forty years was a bit peculiar. Others would have made the journey in less than a month by heading in the right direction.

We stopped half an hour with some Bedouin. There

was no such thing as a loo and the Brig's wife and I learned the art of disappearing behind boulders or hiding in the cleft of a rock (as Moses had done when hiding from God). Bedouin life was harsh, magnificent in its simplicity and totally impossible to imagine as a permanence. Whilst revelling in it for the moment, the thought of returning to our five star luxury in a few days made roughing it for the time being enjoyable.

The Bedouin men crouched around a small fire on which they boiled a kettle. They were clad in their robes or long shirts, with red and white check or plain white keffiyehs either wrapped around their heads or hanging loose with the black aghal around the crown. When tea was made we sipped it from small glasses, and sat on cushions within a rigged up shelter supported by the trunks of palm trees and lined with colourful striped rugs.

Harry peered suspiciously at his small glass which to him (and to me) was lethally germ-infested. He gave his a surreptitious wipe, then a surreptitious spill. It didn't matter as the Bedouin were chatting together in a group outside our shelter. About a hundred yards away their camels rested in the by now hot midday sun. When we wandered over to them, a small boy was shredding a cardboard box and feeding it to his camel who chewed it with aloof satisfaction. I found the beasts astonishing as their back legs, as well as their front ones, were in kneeling positions so that their cloven hooves were turned skywards.

We were driven to a look-out point from which there was a view to a distant oasis. It was the Ayun Khudra Oasis and, from where we stood, rock-hewn steps descended to a wide expanse of white desert sand bounded by rocky crags. A caravan of camels was heading at zero speed for the oasis.

"It is one place where they say, when Moses brings the Israelites from Egypt, they camp here in Sinai," said Zayeed.

"Makes the Bible come alive seeing those camels! Sound of Music stuff but in the desert," remarked the Brig. "Can we walk across to the oasis?" he asked.

Zayeed smiled patiently. "It is too far for you to walk," he replied. "If we have the time we drive there when we return in two days."

We continued our journey, stopping briefly to examine early Christian rock inscriptions, before carrying on along miles of desert road, passing only the odd acacia tree, till we arrived at the Feiran Oasis with its walled-in area of date palms.

"This also is a place where the Israelites they stay," said Zayeed. "Ten years ago, there is much trouble here because there is a deluge and very much is destroyed. You see around the many ruined houses? This happens when it rains so much there is too much water for the wadi."

"Do you get much rain?" asked the Brig.

"Here in Sinai? Five, six times each year. But when it comes there is very much rain for the day. After that nothing. But here they have another problem because the water-level of the oasis it goes down, and the date palms they begin to die."

He led us through an entrance to an early Christian convent, whose small complex contained an old church and a modern one. There were now only two nuns attached to the convent, and both were absent as they were visiting the great Monastery of St. Catherine where we too were going.

In the early centuries of Christianity, ascetics and pious

fanatics had fled from persecution to these desert sites to get close to the Almighty. Sinai had become a popular escape for such people because of its Biblical connections. The Feiran Oasis was a focal point for many anchorites who lived in caves, or built themselves stone shacks on the high rocky hills around the oasis. The grandeur of the Sinai from which it was felt power and spiritual energy could be tapped, was a good setting for searchers after such things.

There had been a central church to which the ascetics had come down from their caves on Saturday evenings for a communal Liturgy. After receiving communion in the early hours of Sunday, the first day of the week, they then returned to their solitary lives. The Feiran Oasis had had a bishop as early as 400 A.D.

We drove on. We were becoming attached to Zayeed and Abdullah, the driver. Abdullah was never intrusive but always there ready and waiting; he seldom spoke, had great grace and an aura of peaceful detachment. I was wrong to say his eyes were burning coals, they were more like quietly smouldering embers; they watched but never enquired. Later, Zayeed asked us if we would mind if we stopped for a while because Abdullah wanted to say his evening prayers.

I was fortunate to be sitting where I could see this slim robed figure in his jacket and Arab head-dress. He walked a few yards into the desert, faced towards Mecca and quietly, without any sign of self-consciousness, prepared himself for the ritual. He was in no hurry but stood for a while, then bent down and used his hand to scrape away the top desert sand to prepare a small and holy area where he could perform his evening prostrations to Allah. When there is no water for purification sand can be used and, I supposed, this was what he was doing. Having made his preparations, he stood in the evening light, arms out, palms upwards, and then was on his knees bowing to the ground. He completed this the required number of times with such grace and naturalness that, had he had a stadium of cheering spectators, I felt he would have been quite unaware of their presence. Harry's comment, when I mentioned this to him later, was that Abdullah probably had been performing a drill which had been instilled into him since birth. It was just something to be done without any thought.

"Like people crossing themselves in church?"

"Yes. No. Yes. You do it without particularly thinking. You do it as a duty," Harry answered.

"As a duty! That's something I must think about!" I said. But I'd already thought. "A duty to whom? A duty to what?"

"A duty to what you know does exist."

"The holy breath of life?"

"To that, then."

"But it doesn't require prayers or songs of praise or prostrations," I went on. "It needs only silence and acknowledgement."

"Well, there you are, you're acknowledging something!" said Harry. But at that moment no more could be said as we were approaching the high sand-coloured defence walls of St. Catherine's Monastery. Above the thick fortress walls a dome was visible, and towering beyond it was the Jebel Musa (the Mountain of Moses).

The air temperature was in sharp contrast to the heat down by the sea. We were taken down some steps leading from the terrace to the monastery guest-house. Our room was sparsely furnished with beds, a cupboard, dressing-table and lamp. We had our own shower and loo, and a radiator we could switch on but which made little difference to the icy damp chill. Visions of the five star luxury hotel was something I wasn't missing, but was definitely looking forward to returning to.

We met the Brig and his wife for supper in the high ceilinged, cold and draughty restaurant. It could hold many pilgrims but that evening it was nearly empty. We sat wrapped in jackets with our teeth chattering. After twenty minutes a large cold salad was placed on our table.

"Just what the doctor ordered," remarked the Brig.

We all helped ourselves, glad of something to eat. Having finished the salad, which brought the chilled-to-the-marrow to below freezing, we were suddenly given bowls of hot soup. Hot soup! Rolls and butter! We devoured the soup and felt warmer. Then came the main course of hot rice and chicken thighs and vegetables. A feast! The breath of life! Despite the hot food we still felt cold.

Harry and I went to bed wearing all our clothes, and I added a woollen balaclava to my head and hiking socks to the bedsocks on my feet. We both took sleeping pills and I was only dimly aware of an irritating and persistent mosquito that started dive-bombing at dawn. At six we woke refreshed, ready for the trek up the mountain, where Moses was said to have received the ten commandments.

We followed Zayeed along a track behind the monastery to where four wild looking Bedouin stood picturesquely waiting with their colourfully attired and saddled camels. The mountain rose steeply behind them, the monastery with its dome protruding above its defence walls lay to our rear. Another way up the mountain could be done by climbing what were known as the Steps of Penitence. It was a quicker route but required agility, as some of the three thousand seven hundred and fifty rock-hewn steps were more than a yard in depth.

The wild looking Bedouin greeted Zayeed and shook hands. The camels looked haughty as they waited in their kneeling positions for their mounts. The Brig's wife, who was a keen horsewoman, was soon aloft with the words 'Amazing! Quite amazing!' Up went the Brig who complained bitterly that he was hellishly uncomfortable. Then it was Harry's turn. His camel roared and grumbled its objections before he climbed on to it and the camel was then ordered to get up. When it had angrily lurched to its feet, there was nothing for it but to stick with it.

It was then my turn to mount. There was no way I could get up without help and, in an undignified manner, Zayeed and one of the Bedouin managed to hoist me up and onto the saddle. I gripped the thick wooden spindle infront and, with a double lunge forward and back, I found myself on high. It was exciting, it was Sinaitic! Mosaic! Ten commandic! I made up adjectives to describe it.

The silence of the camels' feet as they plodded up the track surprised me. For some reason my camel driver walked behind and I depended on my animal having the sense to follow after the others. I'd read that camels were witless beasts who, once facing a direction, went blindly on their way regardless. Mine had a habit of plodding head in air towards the precipice and, only when its head and neck were over it, did it deign to swing around and re-position itself on the track. Once it had done this several times I stopped worrying. Every so often it felt the urge to gather speed so broke into a sort of run. There was little chance of falling off as the thick spindle in front and behind held me in place. "Just relax!" called the Brig's wife, turning in her saddle expertly. "Just let yourself go with the animal's rhythm!"

The experience reminded me of the Prophet Muhammed's camel, Qaswa. Qaswa had been responsible for certain key moments in Muhammed's life, and was believed by Muhammed to be under the guidance and the will of Allah. On his arrival at Medina, for instance, Qaswa had suddenly lain down on some wasteland used for drying dates, and had refused to budge. Muhammed had interpreted this to mean that the place was where he was to live and build his mosque.

So there Muhammed was at Medina, thanks to Qaswa and the will of Allah, and here was I similarly mounted on a camel - come on, swing around, you idiot! That's better! Thanks! - being accompanied by Muhammed's devotees of today: I, a mounted atheist, prepared for enlightenment but receiving not a wit of it, with fellow Christian companions, possibly quite unenlightened too but taking Christianity on trust, heading at this zero speed, but steadily climbing this mountain, at the top of which Moses had received the ten commandments on tablets of stone from the Almighty. It was all fascinating stuff.

My camel driver hooked a transistor onto my saddle. It was playing Arabic music which had a repetitive theme and, having picked up the tune, I began to sing with the joy of the moment. The Sinai peaks as I looked around and let my Qaswa carry me upwards, were not ginger-brown as they'd appeared when flying over the peninsular (was it only two days ago?) they were a strange conglomeration of grey and dark brown sandstone, some with dark copper seams running through them. There were no trees, the whole being an arid wilderness except for tufts of scrub.

The Bedouin of the area were the Jebelya tribe ('jebel' meaning 'mountain'). The word Bedouin comes from the Arabic word for desert, 'baddayah', and a person who lives in it is 'baddawy'. According to a keen young Egyptian, who tried to be helpful and give me information on Sinai, before Christianity the Bedouin of the area had worshipped the Greek goddess of the moon, Sini. This was blatantly untrue as there was no Greek goddess called by that name. There was, however, a Babylonian god of the moon named Sin. According to the Encyclopaedia Britannica 'sin' means 'moon' (it doesn't say in which language) and the connection has been made between 'sin' and the word Sinai. When the Monastery of St. Catherine was built in the sixth century, the Bedouin then abandoned their worship of Sin and became Christian. Afterwards, with the coming of the Moslems in the seventh century, they switched to the more simple Moslem faith which had no complicated Trinity.

We arrived at a stone-built hut manned by the Jebelya who, according to Zayeed, came up daily from their village to sell refreshments and trinkets to pilgrims. First I had to descend from my mount. Forward lurch, pause, then backward lurch as the hind legs went into their kneeling position. How to get off? Well, it was a good question. I was assisted by strong Bedouin arms and lifted bodily into the air and over the spindles. Oh, well, a little indignity and humility were no bad thing. But it was the end of my ride, and I felt sad as I'd quite fallen in love with my camel. I stood by its head and admired its tranquil and beautiful eyes fringed by thick eyelashes and darkened with what in an Arab woman would have been kohl. It had fantastic nostrils which closed like purses to keep out the sand; and the inside of its ears were shaded dark grey and 'wondrous furry' like the ears of Bottom in A Midsummer Night's Dream. There was a quality and sturdy, quiet resignation to its lot which made me feel it had a Qaswa message for me. Fulfil your destiny and don't ask questions about things beyond your mental ability. Keep going; carry your load and don't turn nasty whilst doing it.

"How did you get on?" Harry was smiling triumphantly.

"Marvellous!" I replied. "And none of the things we'd been warned about, like camels being smelly and horrible."

"I'm not getting on one of those brutes again," announced the Brig as he joined us. "One of my more painful experiences and I've had quite a number of them!"

"Isn't this amazing? Look at the view!" the Brig's wife was ecstatic. The Brig raised his binoculars and we took turns to gaze across the mountain ranges. A convoy of quails was spotted nearby making its way through the scrub; nearer still on a stone wall were a couple of small birds, all black except for white tips to their wings and white tails; there were also other small pink finch-like birds. We were given mint tea before we carried on. From there we had to continue on foot.

After we'd walked a little way, we passed a rough path leading down to a flat area with a chapel and cypresses. That, Zayeed told us, was known as Elijah's Plateau. It was where the prophet had come in the ninth century B.C. when fleeing from Jezebel and King Ahab of Israel. Jezebel had been beside herself with rage when Elijah warned her of God's wrath because she and Ahab worshipped Baal. The crunch came when she'd been unable to get Baal to get her sacrificial fire alight however hard she beseeched him, whereas in contrast Elijah had called on God who'd obliged instantly.

Eventually our path joined up with the Steps of Penitence, the final seven hundred or so of which we had to climb. I was less interested in the penitence part than on concentrating on the unevenness of the ground in order not to twist an ankle.

When we crested the last step we came up onto the summit, a relatively broad and flat area, beyond which was a sea of mountains. Zayeed led us to a cave which, he informed us, was the Cave of Moses - the cleft in the rock in which Moses had hidden himself from God's presence. On the summit were also a chapel and a mosque, but both were locked. "It is good that you remember that it is here the religion of the Jews, the Christians and the Moslems come together," Zayeed told us. "It is because it is here they are united by their prophet Moses and their prophet Elijah." We all felt suitably impressed by his words.

I strolled away from the others and stood at the edge of a sharp precipice from which I looked out over range upon range of mountains to the far distance. I wanted to ponder over what Zayeed had said. I remembered that the giving of the ten commandments to Moses was today celebrated by the Jews at their annual Shavuot festival, held seven weeks after Passover. To me the interesting thing was that the apostles of Jesus were Jews (as Jesus himself had been) and the apostles must have been celebrating their Shavuot when the Holy Spirit descended on them in what was to become known to Christians as Pentecost (fifty days after Easter). For Jews it is held on a Sunday fifty days after the second day of Passover.

I was staring out at the panoramic view mulling over these great happenings, when Zayeed wandered over with Harry and the others. He pointed to a higher mountain and told us it was known as St. Catherine's Mountain. It was to that mountain that her body had been borne from Alexandria by angels, after her martyrdom there at the beginning of the fourth century.

St. Catherine had been a young, brilliant and beautiful aristocrat who, living in Alexandria as she did, had studied philosophy, rhetoric, physics, mathematics, astronomy, medicine, you name it and she'd studied it. She'd been brought up a pagan but had become a Christian at the time when the Emperor Maxentius had been persecuting Christians.

St. Catherine admonished Maxentius publicly for sacrificing to the gods, and he in his turn ordered fifty brilliant philosophers to argue with her against Christianity. This they did but with no success, as this scholarly young woman had an answer to everything. Infuriated by this, the Emperor had the hapless philosophers burned alive, and he tried to break Catherine on a spiked wheel (a wheel to which nails and pointed knives were attached), but she had remained unhurt and the wheel had fallen apart hurting only the spectators. Her example of faith brought about the conversion of several hundred soldiers whom the Emperor, by now completely beside himself with rage, ordered to be beheaded. St. Catherine was also beheaded and from her, instead of blood, came milk.

Zayeed said: "You may wish to notice that her mountain is higher than this one. They say it is because God, or Allah, chose the smaller of the two mountains for giving his commandments, to show how much value he places on humility. There is no part of his creation that is beneath his great mercy. When the ten commandments come from God to Moses on this mountain, then all the flowers they come out on the mountain."

The Brig leaned towards me and in a stage whisper said: "Can you remember any of the ten commandments? I can only remember 'Thou shalt not covet thy neighbour's ass', which isn't very difficult to obey as my neighbour hasn't got an ass. Got a wife, but not an ass."

"Darling!" came the rebuke. "Where are your binoculars?"

"Round my neck where they always are."

"Can I borrow them?" The voice was verging on the severe. After years of marriage she knew how to vary her tone so that the Brig got the message when he was overdoing his repartee.

Harry, who had no sense of the sublimity of this holy site, asked me if I was feeling cold. The answer was that yes, I was, but I hadn't noticed it till that moment. The wind up there was a howling cold gale and we'd put on our anoraks to keep out the blast. Zayeed told us it would be tactful to buy refreshments from a wooden shack up there manned by the Bedouin. We were glad to get out of the wind, and sat inside where we could hear it buffeting around; draughts caught at the colourful rugs lining the walls causing them to flap noisily.

Harry asked me to ask Zayeed if they got a lot of people up there normally. He replied that yes, there were often very many - too many. We were fortunate as on Sundays (and it was a Sunday) the monastery was closed to visitors, and tour groups tended not to come then. Their favourite time was at night so that visitors could see the sunrise.

"So we've been lucky we're not surrounded by a mob of tourists, then? Wouldn't want to be climbing those Steps of Hell with others going up and down passing me all the time. Not much room for two, let alone a coach load."

I went out again to look out over the precipitous edge to the range of mountains beyond. In the Old Testament the mountain was said to be endlessly rumbling with thunder. There hadn't in fact been only ten commandments, but hundreds of them ad infinitum regarding clothes, the making of the Ark, the tabernacle, circumcision, food taboos - chapter after chapter of them, until it was difficult not to fall asleep with boredom, certainly to wonder why the Almighty found such detailed instructions important.

Having given his commandments, God then told Moses to go down to his people carrying his tablets of stone. Moses had been forty days and nights up there. Forty seemed to be a magic number as Elijah also fled into the wilderness forty days and nights, and Jesus too went into the wilderness where he was tempted by the devil forty days and nights.

When Moses returned to his Israelites he found them worshipping their newly made golden calf. He was enraged that they could relapse to such idolatry in his absence, and smashed the tablets on which were the ten commandments written with God's finger. What a dilemma! God in his anger wanted to destroy all his Israelites, but Moses quite reasonably argued that if he did, he would be breaking his own promise to Abraham that his descendants would inherit the land he'd promised them. Besides, Moses argued, it was unreasonable to have put him through the task of bringing his Israelites out of Egypt only to destroy them all. Moses actually had the temerity to reprimand God who himself repented. God then commanded Moses to see that only those who took part in the calf-worship were killed. As a result three thousand met their death. Afterwards, Moses had to climb the mountain again to get a second set of tablets. Up and down and up - he must have been strong and bursting with good health.

The Brig came stumping towards me. "Thinking ten commandments?" he asked. "We're thinking lunch. We're all hungry."

Zayeed joined him with his quiet smile. "There is food waiting for us at the first hut," he said. "We go down now?"

"Good man."

We turned away from the wide, sweeping vista of rocky crags and the higher Mountain of St. Catherine, and left the wind-swept summit to begin the long trek down the Steps of Penitence.

A pre-arranged hygienically prepared picnic lunch, suitable for delicate European stomachs, was waiting for us at the Bedouin stone shack half way down the mountain. By this time there was more cloud than blue sky and I substituted the straw hat I'd been wearing for my woollen balaclava.

By the time we finally reached the bottom of the mountain the clouds had blown away and the sky was clear again. There was something magical about the landscape and I hung back to allow the others to get ahead. I sat on a boulder with a note pad and pen, and tried to capture the moment on paper. I was alone in the wilderness.

Firstly, there was the silence.

I sat on my boulder wrapped in the silence with the sun low in the sky to the west, casting a brilliant light on the towering rocks to the east. The wide rock-strewn plateau to the west had sun-rays beaming down on the distant fortress walls and the rising dome of the monastery. It was as if it were a back-drop to a fresco of the Transfiguration. Nearer to me were towering, darkly shadowed fissured rocks. Grey-white clouds wafted above the crags to the north, whilst the southern crags were overlaid by a sort of gauze-like gold transparency.

Sometimes there is a great truth to be faced. God was so up in the air, that nobody wanted to know he definitely didn't exist. It was easier really to stick with God - or at least contain him somewhere in the back of the mind.

Two Bedouin women with five goats came up the rocky slope. They both wore black over ankle length garments, one over bright blue, the other over scarlet. Yashmaks covered the lower half of their faces but revealed very beautiful youthful eyes. They were accompanied by four gleaming black silky-haired goats and one silky-white one. They were very much a part of the Sinai landscape.

"Ah, there you are!" It was Harry who'd retraced his steps to look for me.

"I'm just enjoying the silence! Come and sit for a bit."

"We can't stay, they're all waiting for us."

"Oh, well." Reluctantly, I got up and Harry and I descended the rocky path to join the others.

The Church of St. Catherine is Greek Orthodox and autocephalous. It is, in fact, the smallest independent Church of the Orthodox faith. Only monks of Greek origin (usually from Mt. Athos, the Holy Mountain in north-east Greece) enter its community. The head is the Abbot who also holds the title of Archbishop of Sinai.

Zayeed asked a monk seated out on the terrace

whether I could attend the early morning Liturgy the next day. I watched him conversing with the portly middle-aged, black-bearded figure in his black cassock and monk's head-dress. The face was florid, his eyes a little rheumy and without expression. I thought he looked lifeless, as though he were fighting depression. Having exchanged a few sentences, he remained seated and continued to stare out towards the distant village of St. Catherine and the setting sun. He never once looked in my direction to see who it was wishing to attend the Liturgy.

Yes, Zayeed told me when he returned from the solitary and morose looking monk, if we knocked at 6 a.m. on the door to the outer wall of the monastery, then we'd be admitted. Neither Harry nor the Brig were enthusiastic at the thought of an early rise, but the Brig's wife agreed to join me.

When I went to wake her at five the next morning it was still dark, but with the first suggestion of dawn; the morning star twinkled brightly above the buildings. At five fifty-five when we set off for the church, the star had gone and the craggy mountains were silhouettes; the leaves and branches of a nearby tree were like black lacework against the dawn sky.

We went up from our 'cells' to the terrace where we found a solitary, rather batty looking woman with white hair shaped like a flat beret on her head, wearing hiking attire and carrying a climbing stick. She approached us gesticulating miserably, and we stopped to find out what her problem was. Any word she said dissolved into tears and incomprehensible gibberish. "Oh, oh, oh - "

The Brig's wife put a hand on her shoulder and led her to a chair (one of many on the terrace where refreshments could be enjoyed). One of the monastery Bedouin servants came out, and the Brig's wife astutely passed the hysterical woman into his charge.

"Poor woman's quite lost," she said to me as we walked away.

"You don't think she's quite batty?" I asked.

"No, she's quite lost, poor thing."

For quite some time we knocked on the ancient door in the massive defence walls without any response. Then a nun in a billowing black habit came hurrying across the flagged courtyard, key in hand. Without saying a word she unlocked the door and led us along flagged corridors. Eventually she let us into the dark monastery church and indicated to us to sit in side pews at the back.

There were only five monks present and the chanting was surprisingly quiet. Massive chandeliers hung from the horizontal beams in the ceiling over the nave. Had there been better lighting we might have been able to see the sixth century carvings on the beams which were the originals from the time of the Emperor Justinian.

The chandeliers were not switched on but glinted darkly in the dim light shed from four tall candles placed before the seventeenth century sanctuary screen. A few other candles also flickered in this otherwise unlighted church. The twelve white columns with their black capitals rose from the geometrically patterned mosaic floor; they supported arches to the upper whitewashed wall in which were rectangular windows. The famous apse mosaic of the Transfiguration of Jesus with Moses and Elijah was hidden behind the line of hanging chandeliers.

As the gentle chanting continued, the light increased from the windows and cast grey shadows. A bearded figure dressed in rich ecclesiastic garments censed the church. This was followed by a monk circling the nave holding up the Gospels. One of the monks occasionally chanted a solo and, when he did so, switched on a small shaded lamp on his lectern. When he finished, he switched it off again as if it were vital not to waste one watt of electricity. But the semi-dark added a certain mystery to the occasion.

I was sorry I couldn't see the Transfiguration in the apse. It was said to be superb. And, of course, it was an apt subject for the mountain where both Moses and Elijah had been. Maybe Jesus as a baby had come this way with Mary and Joseph when fleeing into Egypt from King Herod?

So what of God? If he was real and true and full of mercy, then it was amazing. If, on the other hand, he was a figment of man's desperate need for such a deity, then the fact that one had materialized, even if a delusion, was equally amazing!

Man had the ability to imagine anything. It didn't make something less true because it was created in the imagination. An imagined God was as much a consolation - well, even more of a consolation - as he could be imagined merciful. And a God created in man's imagination explained why he couldn't prevent natural disasters, accidents, ill health and death. Man's refusal to accept death as final was a good reason to create God.

These were unsuitable thoughts whilst in this great monastery. Maybe I was satan's pawn, insidiously spreading evil. Or were they merely questions - was one not to question anything?

As the gentle chanting continued, my mind shifted to the Satanic verses in the Koran. Muhammed had been anxious to get the Meccan pagans on side regarding Allah (their al-Lah). Apparently, during one of his moments of enlightenment, Satan had got a look in and Muhammed revealed that the three goddesses, the daughters of al-Lah (al-Lat, al-Uzza and Manat), could be called upon to intercede between men and Allah. This was a terrific boost to the Meccan tribes who felt happy that their pagan goddesses were not being spurned. They felt more able to take Muhammed's monotheism seriously if they could give their goddesses some part to play. But soon Muhammed was enlightened yet again and told that in no way were these three goddesses to be acknowledged. They were nothing but figments of the imagination and not worth a row of beans. 'They are but names which you and your fathers have invented: God has vested no authority in them... Numerous are the angels in the heavens; yet their intercession shall avail nothing until God gives leave to whom He accepts and chooses.' (Sura 53:20)

Standing in the gloomy light of the few flickering candles, but with the sun rising outside, the thought of Harry and the Brig being up and dressed and rearing to get on with the day began to worry me. I whispered in the ear of the Brig's wife, and we slipped away unobtrusively.

We found the hysterical white-haired woman now seated with several kindly, solicitous individuals. She had calmed down and was drinking coffee. The Brig's wife went up and had a word with one of her companions. She learned that the woman was from Finland and had got left behind by her tour guide who was leading a group of Finnish pilgrims up the Mountain of Moses to see the sunrise. How on earth could a tour guide be so careless? Or, perhaps, the woman was habitually late for everything and she was being taught a lesson? The sun always rose on time and if she didn't, well, on this occasion nobody could wait.

'And he was transfigured before them, and his face shone like the sun, and his garments became white as light' (Matthew 17:2). We were at last able to see the mosaics of the Transfiguration in the apse of the church. They were impressive and were original to its sixth century construction, or so I understood from Zayeed. Jesus stood at its centre with Moses and Elijah on either side and, at his feet Peter, John and James. The whole apse mosaic was surrounded by medallions containing the faces of the apostles and the prophets.

I would have liked to have been allowed to browse and take it slowly around the church, but the Brig (and all of us, for that matter) was hoping to have time to visit the Ayun Khudra Oasis which we'd glimpsed from our vantage point several days ago.

Zayeed took us to the charnel-house where, behind a wire netting partition (not unlike a large rabbit-hutch), were piled high the skulls of all the monks who'd died over the centuries. I supposed we were encouraged to look at these macabre mortal remains in order to be reminded that their souls were in Paradise. A sixth century hermit monk, St. Stephanos the Sinaite, was given pride of place, and his skull peered horribly from his ecclesiastical hood and robes. He'd spent his life in a shack beneath the peak of the Mountain of Moses. Personally, I regarded the skulls as loathsome spectacles with nothing to rejoice over. Souls in heaven? I wasn't so sure, but a vision beyond the reality was better than the reality.

The small church, built by St. Helena in the fourth century, and now a chapel at the east end of the katholikon (the main church of an Orthodox monastery), wasn't open to the public. It had been built over the burning bush from which God had first spoken to Moses. This mother of Constantine had had a positive nose for sniffing out holy relics and establishing Christian sites.

"This is the burning bush," remarked Zayeed, stepping back in a small courtyard to allow us to get closer to a magnificent tall shrub with small green leaves on weeping branches, the lower parts of which were stripped of their leaves. "It will grow nowhere else, only here," Zayeed went on. "They try to take cuttings but without success." We were all suitably impressed by his words. But it wasn't the burning bush over which St. Helena's church had been built. That bush had been vandalized by Christians who'd lopped off twigs and leaves and taken them off as holy relics. This was another bush rooted outside - well, maybe from a cutting of the original.

"Where is the mosque?" I asked Zayeed. I particularly wanted to see the mosque built within the thick protective walls surrounding the monastery buildings. It had apparently been built by the monks in a great flurry of speed (said to have been in twenty-four hours) in order to stave off the threat of a Moslem attack in the eleventh century. The erection of the mosque had involved the demolition of the monastery's old original guest-house.

Zayeed pointed down an alleyway to a bell-tower crowned by a cross and, adjacent to it, the minaret of the mosque. But there was no time for a closer inspection, and visitors weren't allowed to enter the mosque anyway, as it was kept exclusively for Moslem guests and the Bedouin servants who worked for the monks.

One of the priceless possessions of the monastery which we were to see displayed in the museum, was a document said to have on it the hand-print of Muhammed (this was his signature) giving his agreement that he would protect the monks of St. Catherine's holy monastery. This, apparently, was in response to a Christian delegation sent to Medina in 625 A.D asking for Muhammed's patronage. The document agreed to their request and made them exempt from paying tax. It is believed that Muhammed had once visited the monastery when on a journey as a merchant for Khadija, his first wife.

Long after his first wife's death, when he'd exiled himself from Mecca to Medina with his devotees, Muhammed occasionally, in order to get some form of livelihood, resorted to banditry, and ambushed camel trains carrying merchandise along the trade routes. He made amends for these desperate forays by distributing whatever surplus loot there was to the needy - he was a sort of Robin Hood but, far from being content with one Maid Marianne, Muhammed had taken to himself thirteen. After the death of Khadija (his first wife, a widow, and many years his senior) he collected wives as a virtuous act. One of them, Aisha (many years his junior), joked that Allah often seemed to do Muhammed's bidding. On one occasion, when he'd managed conveniently to marry the wife of his adopted son with whom he'd fallen in love, the matter became legitimized by Sura 33 in which God sanctioned his love: '...We gave her to you in marriage, so that it should become legitimate for true believers to wed the wives of their adopted sons if they divorced them. God's will must needs be done...' (Sura 33:37)

"You are all finished here now?" asked Zayeed, not wishing to hurry us, but clearly impatient to get going. I felt I was only just beginning, but knew it was the turn of the others who were keen to visit the Ayun Khudra Oasis.

We left the monastery stronghold. The Brig counted

thirty-seven coaches in the monastery car park. Yes, that was amazing! So many pilgrims intent on visiting the biblical site which was also mentioned in the Koran. Groups led by pious priests in dog-collars, or bishops with bejewelled crosses on their breasts. Every nationality disgorged by the coach-load, then borne away again. Pilgrims feeding off the pastures of legend, a touch of truth stirred well with the imagination and made factual by the printed word.

The following day was one to wallow in five star luxury again, and to assimilate all that we'd seen and done over the past few days. It was a balcony-day and an idle-by-the-swimming-pool-day.

Our trip to the Ayun Khudra Oasis had entailed an hour's drive across white desert sand. Abdullah knew the rules of desert driving and, instead of following in the tracks left by former vehicles, zig-zagged at speed across them in order not to sink into the sand.

The encampment had consisted of tents and awnings surrounded by majestic palm trees. The Bedouin men had lounged at ease on cushions whilst the women worked. A number of children of all ages had drawn near with interest. They should have been at school, Zayeed told us, but they could see no point to it. Desert lore was all they needed to learn. A Bedouin infant had come crawling through the sand towards us but had soon been snatched up and carried on the hip of a young ten year old girl. We'd been strange creatures of wonder from another world.

Zayeed had told us something about their medical facilities. All that was required could be found in the desert, he'd said, and there was a local medicine-man who would treat most ailments with extractions from plants. If a hospital was needed then they would have to go to Cairo.

Now at our hotel it was also a catching-up-on-the-world-news-day. We learned from the World Services that the Americans had dropped a bomb or fired a missile somewhere in Iraq and six civilians had been killed. Saddam Hussein was shown on the box bragging that, if attacked, the Iraqis would win a glorious victory by faith.

Tony Blair was also there speaking passionately with his neck muscles knotted and his jaw set. He was sincere in his conviction that this - that that - We'd heard it so often over the past weeks, we ceased to listen. "Do you pray together?" he'd been asked after he'd returned from a meeting with President George W. Bush. Both men were known to be deeply devout Christians. With smiling contempt, Blair had replied, "No, we don't pray together!"

Whether they did or didn't it seemed incredible that they'd got locked into this war situation. Whilst they made passionate declarations, Saddam Hussein remained defiant and unruffled. If Allah had helped Moslems win battles in the past then, surely, he would help again?

The Battle of Badr in 624 A.D., for instance, had been won by a small band of Moslems aided by multiple angels sent by Allah. The victory had been seen as a great salvation and was compared to God's intervention with his Israelites when he'd drowned the Egyptians pursuing them across the Red Sea.

Yet the Almighty wasn't the only deity to give assistance in battle when he chose to, pagan gods and goddesses were also known to have produced miracles of deliverance. For example, the goddess Demeter had been said to raise a cloud of dust over the Greeks, thus confusing the Persian enemy into supposing a far greater army was being fought than there had been. Apollo too was believed to have sent boulders crashing down on the enemy from the towering rocks at Delphi, crushing the invaders and causing the rest of them to flee. There were always wonders to be experienced and turned into truths by the faithful.

It was also a have-to-get-more-money-day. We were down to our last few Egyptian pounds and I needed to change some travellers' cheques. The hotel reception directed me to a small booth down a narrow passageway. There a single bank clerk was seated in what was little more than a broom cupboard, with an open shutter through which transactions could be made. The bank clerk was a pleasant young man in his forties and, because there was no one else wanting to get money, we began to talk. I told him that in England anyone working in a bank would be behind bullet-proof glass, and how nice to do business face to face. He replied pleasantly that that was because there was very little crime in Sharm el-Sheikh.

Was he from Sharm? No, he came from a village near to Luxor, but there were no jobs to be had there and he had had to leave. This somehow led on to the subject of morals and religion and family life which shifted to Islam and Christianity.

Had he done the hajj, I asked? No, he hadn't the money to do it yet, he said sadly, but his brother who was a doctor had. Allah would provide when the time was right, he went on. He seemed so charming and alone and ready to speak, that I couldn't resist asking him what he meant by Allah. It was one of those rare moments when two people become locked together discussing a subject and all else is obliterated.

"He is eternal, everlasting - he has always been and

will always be," came the reply.

"You mean he is a sort of holy spirit?" I asked.

"No, that is not what I mean. Of course Allah is holy. But you pray to Allah because he cares for you. You pray for his goodness and his guidance when it is needed. And, of course, you must not forget to thank him for the things you have."

He had a charming way of slowly nodding his head and watching me with his large brown eyes to see my reaction to his words.

"So what about accidents and misfortunes?" I asked.

"You accept your misfortune and you ask Allah's help to endure it. But always you must thank him for his mercy."

"It sounds - well - " I was going to say 'soothing' or 'therapeutic' but, instead, I used a word which he would understand: "Good," I said.

"It is Islam. It means 'submission'. We are part of Ummah, the great family of Islam."

Locked together in eye contact between Moslem and atheist was strangely harmonious and prompted me to ask: "So what about Satan?"

"Excuse me? What is the word 'Satan'?"

I remembered the Arabic: "Iblis," I said.

"Ah, Iblis! Always you must drive away Iblis. You call on Allah to help you so that only it is Allah who is with you. You have to understand that when a Moslem greets a friend, he begins by saying, 'Peace be on you', and the friend will say the same. This creates a bond of peace and the protection of God."

"It's so simple," I remarked.

The charming Egyptian with his large brown eyes who was sagely nodding his head at me, went on: "It is important to know that Moslems are not a threat. So many people in Europe they are afraid of Islam and think we want to make the world Moslem. This is not true. All we want and pray for is that we have justice." The subject shifted swiftly and unexpectedly to Israel and Palestine and the injustice of the situation there. American support of Israel and his eyes immediately grew hard. The mood change was startlingly swift. My own thoughts were that here was a forty year old who was charming and intelligent, but there was a flash-point where it was essential to change the subject fast, or make a quick get-away. With his eyes rolling he was beginning to talk so fast that I was unable to pick up on what he was saying anyway. When at last he paused, I somehow managed to turn the topic back to peace, and I asked him to write down on the back of my travellers' cheque receipt the words in Arabic for 'Peace be on you'. The showing-the-whites-of-his-eyes maniac spitting fury from his cubby-hole, quickly controlled his features and became the large brown-eyed and charming Egyptian again as he wrote the words. When he had finished, and whilst we were both once more in harmony, I quickly smiled and read the words he'd written: "Salaam al-laykum," I said, and fled.

"That'll teach you not to talk about Islam with Moslems," said Harry, when I told him of this minor fracas.

"It wasn't Islam that created the hiatus," I objected, "it was Israel and Palestine."

"Well, there you are! Just keep off the subject, that's all I'm saying," said the wise one.

Which left me still wondering whose side God was on under such circumstances.

We were once more on camels, quietly plodding along flat desert sand between rocky crags. We were on our way to a Bedouin feast. It was late afternoon and we were getting another taste of desert life, enjoying the flavour without having to endure it.

I thought I might have cracked a rib when mounting this camel, my new Qaswa. Zayeed had grasped me around the midriff and had heaved me up with such strength that something had twanged in the rib area. It was slightly comical as well as slightly painful. The double lunge forward and back when Qaswa had stood up hadn't made it worse, but I was anxious how it'd be when she kneeled down again. I didn't want more double lunging than was necessary.

We plodded on. The sun was low in the sky, casting long camel shadows, and turning the craggy peaks gold in sharp contrast to the darkened lower slopes. Plod, plod, plod - a slow rhythm, advancing to a yet unseen destination hidden amongst the rocky boulders through which we were passing.

The tall Bedouin teenager who was leading my animal stopped to allow the others to catch up. I was afraid Qaswa without warning might decide to lie down. The Prophet's Qaswa had staged another sit-in when Muhammed had decided in March 628 A.D. to make the hajj pilgrimage to Mecca. He thought that if he performed this ancient custom, it would be an act of reconciliation with the pagan Meccan tribes. He prepared camels for ritualistic sacrifice, shaved the pilgrims' heads and put on the customary white unstitched cloth before setting out for the city. As he and his followers approached Mecca, Muhammed had shouted out, 'Labbayk al-Llahuma Labbayk' (Here I am, Oh God, at your service). Qaswa, however, had had other ideas. Once more she'd lain down and had refused to budge. Muhammed's companions had shouted at her and called her names, but Muhammed himself had seen it as a sign from Allah not to make the hajj that year. He ordered his followers to sit down and be at peace. Reconciliation and not war were to be his tactics. The chief Quraysh tribe had been astonished at this peaceful sit-in, and hadn't dared to violate Meccan custom by attacking those coming on a pilgrimage to the Ka'bah. A treaty was finally drawn up permitting Muhammed and his Moslem followers to perform the lesser hajj in future years, during which time the Quraysh would evacuate Mecca. And, thanks to Qaswa, this was what happened.

We arrived at the Bedouin encampment. To dismount was less of an ordeal than I'd feared. Perhaps my Qaswa sensed I needed a smooth descent and went down with extra care. Our camels were then mounted by the teenage Bedouin guides who, with happy yells, raced away atop their mounts. The gilding thrown from the setting sun onto the craggy mountain tops to the east was superb. The sun, itself a large orange disc, was descending to the horizon in the west. As it sank lower, the nearer crags became black Indian ink silhouettes against the pale gold sky.

And there suddenly I saw the crescent moon.

It was the finest, largest crescent moon I'd ever seen, and rested on its back like a sliver of gold against the pale sky.

The Bedouin in their robes and head-dresses sat cross-legged around a fire over which a large black upturned metal bowl stood; on it they laid a thinly rolled out mixture which was browned and cooked like a large pancake. I noticed another Bedouin seated before a metal tripod and flattening the mixture with a rolling-pin before handing it to the cook. A hubble-bubble stood to one side.

There were greetings, handshakes and 'Salaam al-laykums'. Zayeed led us to where cushions and rugs were laid out on the trunks of palm trees. Paper mugs of sweet tea were handed around with the Arab bread. He then gave us a demonstration of the hubble-bubble and we had a chance to try it. After several attempts, I eventually achieved the bubbling sound, together with a lungful of smoke. It was supposed to produce a feeling of euphoria but, as I'd been feeling euphoric before and now was only choking which hurt my rib, I passed it back to Zayeed.

Candle lanterns were placed in strategic niches on the darkening outline of crags and boulders, giving the scene a mysterious quality. A few stars began to twinkle overhead; the crescent moon was brightening. The Moslem New Year was well and truly underway.

We were summoned to a long trestle table covered with a white cloth where dishes of rice, lamb casserole and barbecued chicken were waiting for us.

"The cooks have been busy in their kitchens. Don't the wives come and join us, Zayeed?" asked the Brig.

"No. They stay with the children," came the answer.

"Where are they?"

"In their village nearby."

"Hm. Their village being a couple of wigwams around the corner?"

"Excuse me? What is wigwam?"

"Tents."

Seated on our palm trunks with our plates of food I asked Zayeed about the Moslem New Year. Their New Year's Day had been the day before, and had been heralded by the first sighting of the new moon. He told me that it was a family affair and not celebrated like certain other festivals with processions, music and dancing.

"But the tenth day of our New Year - Ashura - commemorates many important historical events in Islam," he went on. "For example, the birth of Adam, and the birth of the Prophet Abraham and the Prophet Isa."

"Isa?" I queried.

"To you he is Jesus."

"Ah, yes."

"Have you heard of Husayn, the grandson of Muhammed? It is the day that the Shi'ite Moslems remember his martyrdom at Karbala in Iraq."

"Really?"

"The Shi'ites are in mourning for Husayn for the first ten days of Muharram. Then they have a procession and some of them they beat themselves with chains - is it to flagellate?"

"Yes. We saw his mosque in Cairo when we were there last year. It's there they have his head as a holy relic."

"This you see? You have seen the head?" asked Zayeed.

"No. I wasn't allowed in," I said.

"No, it is not permitted."

"I've read," I went on, "that the mourning for Husayn is sometimes compared with Holy Week in Christianity. Fatimah, his mother, is like Mary, the mother of Jesus, because both mourned for their dead sons."

"I think you like to make these comparisons? You like to see what there is in Islam from Christianity?"

"Or from Judaism."

"And I too read much. You know that at Mecca there are, before Islam, pictures of Jesus and Mary on the walls of the Ka'bah? The word is fres - what is the word?"

"Frescoes?"

"Yes, thank you.   There are frescoes also of many of the pagan gods and goddesses.   And when Muhammed he comes at last to the Ka'bah and performs the first Moslem hajj, he destroys all these pictures except he leaves the frescoes of Jesus and Mary his mother.   Maybe it is because one of his wives is Christian."

"Isn't that interesting!"

It was by now quite dark and many stars spangled the sky, with the crescent moon still a brilliant fine jewel in the heavens. The Sinai crags were black forms shadowed only where the lanterns had been placed. Zayeed was telling me how it was said that the Mountain of Moses in Sinai had once been part of Mount Moriah (the Temple Mount) in Jerusalem. Legend had it that for some reason it had broken away and gone into the wilderness of Sinai. Why, he didn't know, but it made a nice story.

The Temple Mount was where Solomon's temple had stood. Adam, it was said, had been created by God there, and it was there that Abraham had been prepared to sacrifice Isaac. It was there also that great events were expected to take place at the end of time.

One of the Bedouin sitting by the embers of the fire picked up an Arab harp and called Zayeed over to perform on a small drum. He sat cross-legged in the circle around the fire and tucked the drum under one arm, holding it at an angle which enabled him to use both his powerful hands (rib-cracking ones) to beat it. Soon the rhythmic drumming began and was accompanied by the twanging sound of the Arab harp, together with the plucking of a zither-like instrument. Male Bedouin voices and the clapping of hands in time to the music resounded as they sat around their fire, their Arab features lit by the dying flames.   We took our cushions closer to the hearth and warmed ourselves by the fire and joined in the clapping. Every now and then they quadrupled the tempo of the hand claps before returning to the original beat.

"This time tomorrow we'll be home again!" Harry suddenly remarked.

What sacrilege! To talk of home when we were in the Sinai desert with the Bedouin entertaining us! The harp was replaced with a more melodious rustic looking lute. The male voices continued to sing with energy.

After an hour or so of such entertainment Zayeed put down his drum and, getting up, told us to follow him.

"This is where we're taken hostage," confided the Brig. "Retired soldier and wife feared dead after Bedouin ambush. Sort of headline they like in our local rag."

"How does your rib feel now?" asked Harry taking my hand as we followed Zayeed into the blackest of black nights between the barely perceived solid outline of boulders. "Don't worry, I've got you so you won't fall," went on my beloved spouse stumbling over a rock but, fortunately, not taking me with him to the ground but being held up by me instead.

Under the looming blackness of a crag Zayeed told us to lie down and look up at the heavens.   For ten minutes, he said, we were to remain silent.

"What if a wolf comes?" demanded the Brig.

"Shhh!" said his wife.

We did as we were told.

There are moments in life which become indelibly stamped on the mind.   That night when lying in silence staring up at the night sky was one of them.   The myriad stars, the firmament, the galaxies; the brilliantly burnished crescent moon - the silence -

War? How was war possible? What made men fight? What mania possessed the human spirit to make them want to kill each other?

How strange that all that remained of Solomon's temple at Jerusalem was the Wailing Wall. Strange too that in 135 A.D. the Emperor Hadrian had had a temple of Jupiter built on the site. Then away with that for Christian Byzantine churches. Then came the victorious Moslems and up went the Dome of the Rock and the al-Aqsa Mosque. But the Crusaders weren't having that and recaptured Jerusalem, if only briefly, and converted the al-Aqsa to a Christian church in 1099 A.D. But oh, no! back came the Moslems. The Crusaders went willingly to battle believing that if they were killed they would become martyrs, just as today Moslem suicide bombers believe themselves martyrs.

The Dome of the Rock encloses exactly what it says, the rock - THE rock where Adam was fashioned. THE rock where Abraham (neither Jew nor Christian nor Moslem) was willing to submit to the will of Almighty God. And it was there from THE rock that Muhammed made his night journey and went up to the seventh heaven to Allah. And there at THE rock that it is expected on the final Day of Judgement that the black stone set in a corner of the Ka'bah will return to unite with THE rock where a place awaits it. It is thought that the black stone (originally white but which turned black due to the sins of men) was sent down from heaven - not unlike the palladium of the goddess Athena which fell from heaven.

I saw a shooting star. It was a good omen. Perhaps there wouldn't be war with Iraq? Perhaps Saddam Hussein would be assassinated or else step down? What right had America to command and dictate to other countries - to play God? Why didn't God play God when he could or even should on occasions?

Alexander the Great, whose family believed themselves descended from the supreme god, Zeus, had once delivered a speech at a banquet outlining his vision to unite all nations and civilize them by introducing Greek ideals of justice and peace. His own words at the banquet had been: 'I do not distinguish among men... I classify them using only one criterion: virtue... On my part, I shall consider you all equal, whites or blacks, and I wish you would be not only subjects of the commonwealth, but participants and partners... As much as this depends on me, I shall try to bring about what I promised. The oath we made over tonight's libations, hold onto as a Contract of Love.' It has been suggested that Christianity inherited the testament of Alexander the Great.

But then centuries later Muhammed, not long before his death, preached a farewell sermon in 632 A.D. in which he said: '...An Arab has no superiority over a non-Arab; a white has no superiority over a black, nor a black over a white, except by piety and good deeds...' There was a curious similarity between the words of Alexander the Great and the Prophet Muhammed.

Looking up at the firmament and the galaxies and the stars and the crescent moon poised low in the heavens, I found myself thinking there had to be some divine hand holding the constellations under control - guiding, keeping all in motion and not allowing any part of it to get out of harmony. A supreme orchestral conductor controlling the instruments of the heavens.

It wasn't easy being an atheist as doubts and fears kept creeping in through the back door, in fact through all the doors, to my mind. One's brain seemed to be computerized to deity. Perhaps I should just accept belief - well, of a sort.

The muted roar of a distant passenger jet seeped into the silence. Winking wing-lights slowly passed across the heavens until they disappeared behind the towering outline of a boulder. There was nothing that the human mind and brain couldn't create when the seed of an idea was planted and it was given time to germinate.

No wonder out of love and compassion for men, a glorious destination and after-life had been invented. And the invention became an accepted truth. It was a masterpiece of imaginative art. It was vital.

But maybe it wasn't just imagined!

A dark form rose from the desert beside us. "Now it is time," said Zayeed.

"That was quite unforgettable!" said the Brig's wife.

"Trust the airliner to make its crossing at that moment," the Brig remarked.

Harry was full of his sightings of various stars, planets, the Milky Way - The subject of black holes and inter-planetary collisions, nebulae, star clusters and heaven knows what, became the main topic as we groped our way back in the dark.

"We must get a telescope! A book on astronomy and a telescope!"

"Not often you can see the stars at home," grumbled the Brig. "Too much cloud or street lighting. Can't win, can you? You get up at two in the morning to see some eclipse of the moon and it's ruddy well raining. Nothing you can do about it!"

"Have you ever been to England, Zayeed?" enquired the Brig's wife. She was actually walking beside Harry whom she thought was Zayeed in the dark. His voice came from elsewhere. "No. One day I would like very much."

"Come and visit us if you do," said the Brig. "We'll try and give you as good a time as you've given us."

"Thank you."

"We'll give you our phone number before we go."

We returned to the bonfire where the five Bedouin were still sitting cross-legged and chatting around the dying embers. Zayeed said good-bye and shook hands with each in turn. Many 'salaams' were exchanged before we climbed into our Land Rover where Abdullah was waiting for us. As it rattled away, the headlights probed the dark, revealing the desert track between the tall Sinai rocks, and beamed into camel thorn giving it the eerie appearance of dried up table decorations. A jackal, or maybe a fox, was picked up in the beam, its eyes pin-points of light, before it slunk away into the dark. As we gained the main tarmac road and headed back to Sharm el-Sheikh, the stars became barely visible, and the crescent moon was gone.

"Jolly good evening but not a way of life I'd like to live," the Brig declared.

"Maybe ours isn't a way of life they'd like to live," I said.

"Wouldn't want to spend my life in the desert arguing about whose dates belong to whom, or squabbling over a pail of water. Don't suppose anyone knows who owns what out in the desert - all depends on a handshake or a stab in the back."

Our five star luxury hotel informed us we could use our rooms until our departure that afternoon because there were no new arrivals. We found in other parts of the hotel grounds, fountains and waterfalls and a duck pond, a children's playground, a tennis-court and more swimming-pools amongst trees and flower-beds. A real paradise or Garden of Eden.

Of course Adam had to be tempted. What would life be without temptation? An endless turgid, torpid nothingness? What was beauty without ugliness, or joy without sadness? Socrates, without bowing to the Almighty, but suspecting there was only one supreme god, highlighted the phenomenon of contrasts, and went on to say that, because there could be no life without death, so there could be no death without life again. Interesting.

We lounged on our balcony and stared out across the gardens and swimming-pools and palm trees to the Red Sea. All was tranquillity and peace belying the political situation. The World Service that morning had shown another Arab summit held this time in Qatar. The Arab countries were divided over the impending war, and several representatives had had a stand-up fight, one of them shouting furiously at the other, 'May Allah cut your moustache!' In contrast there was an earnest and pious Christian gathering of Church leaders calling for peace. Behind the calls for war and peace, and the cooings and rantings, came the muted message that once Saddam Hussein was got rid of then pressure would be put on Israel to give up its settlements, or at least act more fairly towards Palestine. First things first. War first.

Then peace.

I remained a wavering atheist. But in the same manner of Socrates' wheel of contrasts, there could be no atheism without God. On this revolving wheel I was inevitably going towards belief even when I was moving away.

"So just accept it!" said Harry, when I informed him

of these weighty matters. "You might as well settle for the positive rather than the negative." And he closed his eyes for a last hour's luxury snooze.

I was left to continue mulling over the pros and cons of religion. I couldn't see why, if God existed, he couldn't plant in my mind the right seed of belief as, presumably, he had the power to do anything he chose to. To my way of thinking, if God didn't choose to, then it was hardly my fault if I couldn't really believe in him.

I began to make plans for our next journey. Next destination – Jerusalem.

THE END

GLOSSARY
OF GODS, HEROES AND EGYPTIAN HIEROGLYPHS

AKH

Believed by the ancient Egyptians to be the form by which the deceased was recognized in the underworld. The akh could only result when the deceased's ba had united with his ka. Once this had occurred the akh was created and remained unchanged for eternity.

AL-LAH

The supreme god of the pagan Arabs to whom the Ka'aba in Mecca was originally dedicated. He had three daughters, al-Lat, al-Uzzah and Manat.

AL-LAT

Daughter of al-Lah.

AL-UZZAH

Daughter of al-Lah

AMUN

One of the most important gods in the Egyptian pantheon. The Greeks identified him with Zeus. He was usually depicted as a human figure wearing a double-plumed crown, but was also represented as a ram with curved horns.

AMUN-RA

The combination of the god Amun with Ra the sun-god. It was Amun-Ra who presided over the expanding Egyptian empire in Africa and the Levant.

ANKH

Hieroglyphic sign denoting eternal life. It is not unlike a Christian cross surmounted by a loop and was adopted by the Coptic Church in Egypt.

APIS BULL

The sacred bull who served as the physical manifestation of the god Ptah (creator god).

APOLLO

Greek god of music and prophecy. Also the god of light and once identified with the sun Helios. The dolphin was sacred to him.

ARGONAUTS

Greek heroes who sailed up the Bosphorus with Jason to recover the golden fleece from Colchis on the Black Sea.

ARTEMIS

Twin sister of Apollo. She was goddess of hunting, but also defender of wild animals and children. At Ephesus she was a fertility goddess.

ATHENA

Daughter of Zeus. She was goddess of wisdom.

BA

The Egyptian concept of a man's personality and one of the five essentials making up a person, the others being his physical body, his ka, his name and shadow.
On his death the deceased's ba has to rejoin his ka which then becomes an akh and continues for eternity.

BAAL

A fertility god of Canaan.

BYZAS

Daughter of Poseidon and Cereossa, founder of the small town Byzantium which was to become Constantinople.

CEREOSSA

Daughter of Zeus and Io. She was loved by Poseidon and gave birth to a daughter, Byzas.

CYBELE

The Asiatic great Mother Goddess, goddess of the powers of nature and fertility.

DIONYSOS

Greek god of wine and drama, son of Zeus.

HELIOS

The sun, later identified with Apollo.

HERA

Greek goddess of women and marriage, wife of Zeus.

HERMES

Son of Zeus, and god of wayfarers and merchants. He also conducted the souls of the dead to the underworld.

HORUS

Egyptian god of the sky. He was believed to be the embodiment of divine kingship, and protector of the reigning Pharaoh. He was usually depicted as a hawk or falcon, or as a man with the head of the bird. The Horus-falcon is often shown with outstretched wings behind the head of the king whom he is protecting.

IO

A priestess at the temple of Hera near Argos in Greece. Zeus fell in love with her and in anger Hera changed her into a heifer and set a gadfly on her. It so tormented the poor girl/heifer that she fled all over the world trying to escape it.

ISIS

Egyptian goddess, wife of Osiris and mother of Horus. She was the goddess who encapsulated all the virtues of women, and was the symbolic mother of the Pharaoh as he was regarded as the manifestation of her son, Horus.

JASON

The rightful heir to a kingdom in Thessaly, northern Greece. Before he could win back his kingdom he had to recover the golden fleece.

KA

The creative life-force of every human or divinity. One of the five essentials that make up an individual. On his death a man's ka has to reunite with his ba which then becomes an akh and continues for eternity.

KYBELE

See Cybele.

LETO

A Titaness who was loved by Zeus and gave birth to Apollo and Artemis.

MAAT

Egyptian goddess of truth, justice and the essential harmony of the universe. It was she who presided over the judgement of the dead when the deceased's heart would be weighed against her feather.

MANAT
> One of the three daughters of al-Lah.

NEPHETYS
> Sister of the Egyptian goddess Isis. She was virtuous but was married to the evil Seth.

OSIRIS
> An important god of the ancient Egyptian world, married to Isis. Osiris was associated with death, resurrection and fertility, and was usually depicted as a mummy with his hands protruding holding the royal insignias.

POSEIDON
> Greek god of the sea and earthquakes.

PTAH
> Egyptian creator-god of Memphis, the capital city of the Pharaonic period, some twenty-four kilometers south of Cairo.

RA
> The Egyptian sun-god. He is usually represented as a hawk-headed figure wearing a sun-disc head-dress. When, however, he is sailing in a solar barque in the underworld he is ram-headed.

SERAPIS
> Following Alexander the Great, Ptolemy I introduced a new god, Serapis, who was worshipped in Alexandria. He was a combination of the Egyptian god Osiris, the Apis bull, and several Hellenistic gods, and embodied their various attributes.

SETH

The evil Egyptian god, brother of Osiris. He was god of chaos and was often depicted with a human body but the head of an evil, mysterious beast. He was married to Nephetys, sister of Isis.

SIN

Babylonian moon god.

THOTH

Egyptian god of writing and knowledge, usually depicted as a baboon or an ibis.

TITANS AND TITANESSES

A race of Greek immortals born of Uranus (personification of the heavens) and Gaea (mother earth).

ZEUS

Supreme Greek deity. God of the heavens and the weather. He was the giver of laws and dispensed justice.

REVIEWS OF 'YE GODS!'

An engagingly written travel book with a difference.
The title 'Ye Gods!' at once a description and an exclamation, reveals both agnostic Jill's fascination with old myths and her bemusement by, or perhaps exasperation with, the tenets of the Christian faith. It is this oblique stance that makes the book particularly interesting.

Western Daily Press

Very entertaining. I often laugh out loud while reading – but also very thought-provoking.

Debbie Thrower

There is much to commend about the double act put on by this older British couple as they proceed in leisurely pursuit of the gods through cities and towns to mountains and to islands....

This is a quirky, worthwhile and intelligent book written by an enthusiast.

Athens News

JILL DUDLEY'S
NEXT BOOK
'YE GODS AGAIN!'
CONTINUING ON FROM
'YE GODS!'